THE COMPASSION BOOK
Lessons from The Compassion Course

*For anyone who wants more compassion
in their life and in our world*

THOM BOND

Please purchase only authorized electronic editions, and do not participate
in or encourage electronic piracy of copyrightable materials.
Published by ONE HUMAN PUBLISHING.
Orange Lake, NY 12550

ISBN: 978-0-9994411-1-4

This book is dedicated to my friend and mentor, Marshall Rosenberg. It is my way of sharing his inspiration and ideas – a bell I intend to ring for the rest of my life.

ACKNOWLEDGEMENTS

Patricia – who taught me about life

Nirjhari – who taught me how to write when it mattered most

Kumari – who knew I could finish this before I did

My Compassion Course partners – Antonio, Clara, Gabi, and Shahinaz, thank you modeling love and leadership – thank you for hope.

Welcome To The Book

In the same way that we humans have developed our knowledge and understanding of the physical world, we have also developed our knowledge and understanding of compassion. This book was created to share this with you.

Through clear, specific ideas, and practical steps, this book provides you with the "how to" of compassion. By developing foundational skills, and building on them over time, we experience more compassion on a daily basis – and that changes everything.

Each chapter features a concept, a story to illustrate the concept, and practices that help us put that concept into action.

Although the work in this book is readily understandable, putting it into practice can be very challenging. I've done my best to make this something doable and real in your life, something that makes a difference for you and all of us. Your part will be to provide perseverance, practice, focus, and dedication.

Together, we've got this. Here we go!

CONTENTS

CHAPTER I

THE CONCEPT

EVERYTHING WE DO, WE DO TO MEET A NEED

If there is one idea that speaks to the core of compassionate thinking, it is this: Everything we've ever done, everything any human being has ever done, or will ever do, is an attempt to meet a need, or needs (successfully or not). All human acts can be seen as an attempt to meet needs.

From scratching our heads (comfort) – to eating meals (nutrition) – to getting married (partnership) – to yelling at someone (self-expression) – all acts can be seen as an attempt to meet needs.

I do not claim this is true or not true. It is a way of seeing things.

I do claim that when I have this perspective or awareness – when I can see my own actions or the actions of others in a context of universal human needs – I experience more connection and compassion. Seriously, it works.

To be clear, when I say needs I mean more than just the things we can't live without (air, water, food, shelter, clothing, medical care, etc.). I mean all the things that we all want to experience in a full human life.

In compassionate thinking, the reason that needs are so important is that as long as we choose to think about them, we have common ground.

This way of seeing things has changed every relationship I have.

Throughout the book, we will work on refining, defining, and getting clarity about what needs are, how we can see them, deepen our relationship to them and ultimately enrich our lives and the lives of everyone around us.

Check out Appendix B to see a list of needs.

I hope the following story will bring some context, clarity, and hope.

IN PRACTICE

A TALE OF TWO FATHERS

I'll never forget the first time I used this way of thinking in a conversation with my father. After forty years, I was sure that he would never stop criticizing me and telling me what I should do. All my adult life I felt miserable during the holidays, dreading these interactions with my Dad. It was driving me crazy.

I had been studying with my mentor, Marshall Rosenberg, for a little over a year when I visited my parents for Thanksgiving. It wasn't long before I found myself in the living room, face-to-face with my father. He was asking about my immediate plans. It went like this.

Dad: So Thom, how's the organization (NYCNVC) coming along?

Me: Great (feeling a bit apprehensive already). People are getting involved, there's a lot of interest. It seems to be going really well.

Dad: That's great (a moment of silence). Do you have a business plan?

Me: Yes, we do (I wrote business plans professionally at one point).

Dad: Good, because you need a business plan. Is it in writing?

Me: Yes, Dad, it is in writing (I could feel the annoyance rising in me).

Dad: That's great – your business plan needs to be in writing (more silence). Does your plan have a Gant chart? You know, a list of all the things that need to be done, all the people that will do them and exactly when they will get done. Do you have that?

Me: Yes, Dad we do. (Now I was "on edge"). And yes, it's in writing. This felt so familiar – and not in a good way.

The "interrogation" continued. Finally, out it came.

Dad: All the best plans and ideas don't matter, Thom, even if you do get them on paper. You've got to get out there and do it! Thom, you really have to get your act together!

Super Slo-Mo

The moments that followed my father's words were different from any I had experienced with him during the previous forty years. I'd like to share them with you in "super slow motion", in the hope it may contribute to you.

STEP 1

I slowed down. Way down. As they say, if you keep doing what you're doing, you'll keep getting what you're getting. The moment my father "started in", I remembered to slow down so I could choose to act – and not REact. Thanks to my studies in compassionate thinking, I was able to notice three things happening.

1. I had an unmet need.

2. I had a judgment.

3. I was about to get into another fight with my father if I didn't do something different this time.

My challenge was to get centered by focusing on the "unmet need" and not the "judgment". This was a challenge for me, since through-out my life I had learned to blame others for my unmet needs. So my tendency was to focus my attention on blaming rather than focusing on my needs.

In my new practice of compassion, I had been working on catching these moments and slowing down so I could focus on my needs and others' needs, *not* blame or judgment.

To reinforce this new habit, I had given myself some "keys" that would remind me I was going down the path to disconnection again. I noticed a tightening in my chest, and the thought, "he shouldn't be saying that; he's being so critical." That was my cue; tight chest and the "should/shouldn't" thoughts.

STEP 2

I gave myself empathy. I asked myself, "What am I really feeling and needing in this moment?" I was feeling a bit agitated, but also somehow hopeful. I wanted to be seen, I really wanted more ease, and I was yearning for some connection. From this awareness of my needs, I was able to make my choice. I went for connection.

STEP 3

I listened empathically. Next, I tried out my "compassionate ears", ears that heard only my father's needs. This was my moment of truth. In my head I repeated the words, "all acts are an attempt to meet needs. All acts are an attempt to meet needs."

"But what X?$#x! needs", I wondered, could possibly be met for my father, by giving me such a hard time? I asked myself again, "What needs…?" This time I was really starting to wonder.

By genuinely asking myself and wondering, "what needs could he be meeting by talking to me this way?", I was able to see my father's "attack" differently. I was able to see his actions as an attempt to meet needs. I had found a new way to see my father.

It went like this:

"So Dad, it sounds like you really want me to do well out there and you'd love it if I could benefit from your experience. Is that true?"

He looked confused for a moment as he tipped his head to one side. After some silence, in a tone that seemed a combination of relief and delight, he said, "yes… yes it is."

Focusing on my father's needs changed the moment. Right before my eyes, he transformed from a "critical, didactic, know-it-all," to a man who loved his son and wanted to help him succeed.

I'll never forget that moment. I could have defended myself. I could have tried to convince him that I did have my act together. Yet in that moment, I was focused on something else; needs. What seemed most important was that my father wanted to help me, and this was the best way he could think of. From that perspective, I was able to find connection, and for the first time in a long, long time, we weren't fighting.

PRACTICES

PRACTICE 1

Notice Needs – Keep a small journal with you throughout the day. Make 1 to 5 entries per day that include the description of an act or words spoken by someone and what need you imagine they were trying to meet. It is VERY helpful to limit the words you use to those on the Needs List in Appendix B. The reasons for doing this will become clearer in the coming chapters.

PRACTICE 2

Notice Needs (more challenge) – Think of someone who is close to you who is doing or saying something you don't like. See if you can figure out what need they are attempting to fulfill. Again, it is VERY helpful to limit the words you use to those on the Needs List in Appendix B. The reasons for doing this will become clearer in the coming chapters.

CHAPTER 2

THE CONCEPT

WHAT WE WERE TAUGHT

Even though it is possible to see all acts as an attempt to meet needs, most of us were taught something else. Most of us were taught that people do things for other reasons. We were given another way to look at people's actions: An entire category of reasons that we can call "judgments".

RIGHT AND WRONG

Many of us learned that there are "right things" and "wrong things". And that we should do the "right things" and not do the "wrong things".

GOOD AND EVIL

It is still considered a rational explanation of human behavior to attribute "evil" to people's actions. A well-known New York Times editorial writer recently made this case about a shooting in the US.

Many of us also share the notion that certain people or actions are good as well.

SHOULD AND SHOULDN'T

I know for me, this is the most pervasive and difficult form of judgment to recognize. As a small child, I learned to be a human and to fit in by finding out what I "should" or "shouldn't" do.

COMPASSION FOR OUR JUDGMENTS

In the last chapter we explored the idea that "Everything we do, we do to meet a need." This includes using judgments. For example, by labeling certain people as "evil", we know to "stay away or protect from" and that might meet our need for safety. It might also meet a need for *understanding* – why people act as they do.

When I think about judgments in this way, I have a deeper understanding and more compassion for people who are judging (myself included). It is this "needs behind the judgment" thinking that allows me access to my compassion. I no longer feel compelled to judge the "judgers".

So we can see how judgment might help us meet certain needs. That said, it rarely meets needs for connection or engenders compassion.

SO WHY DO I WANT TO KNOW ABOUT JUDGMENTS?

We can look at judgments as being important in two ways. One, they tend to disconnect us from one another, and two (ironically), they let us know about our needs.

For example, imagine someone came up to you and said, "Hey, listen, I'd like to talk to you about how stupid you're being." Would you like to have that conversation? Or would you be put off, maybe shocked? Disconnected?

Now imagine someone came up to you and said, "Hey, listen... I'd like to talk to you about how we can have more flow and communication between us." Would you be interested in that conversation? I imagine it would be more likely.

This example shows a new way to think about all judgments, a way that gives us a more connecting and compassionate view. Think of any judgment word you or someone else might use, and you can match it to something you or they would like and are not experiencing... a need.

"Selfish" – Perhaps more mutuality or consideration?

"Mean" – Perhaps care or understanding?

"Stupid" – Perhaps understanding or effectiveness?

When we use judgment language:

1) We disconnect and are less likely to think about needs.

2) Since we never actually bring specific need(s) into our consciousness, again, we are way less likely to consider them or meet them.

3) It's usually not as much fun as knowing the needs behind it.

When we can notice judgments and translate them into needs:

a) We can talk to people about our own and one another's needs while being more likely to stay in connection.

b) We can create more connection with, and have more compassion for, someone who is in pain.

It can be a great challenge to notice our judgments. Yet, when we learn to notice or have this awareness, we create a foothold for compassion.

So you could say, the skill of *unpacking* or *translating* judgments – to create a clearer understanding of needs, gives us an awareness that is a key to engendering compassion – even in the face of conflict and/ or pain. Awareness of needs also increases the odds of having them met, ultimately increasing our happiness and compassion as well.

Noticing and translating judgments is one of the greatest challenges in the realm of compassionate thinking, and yet offers some of the greatest benefits.

I invite you on a journey toward this awareness and to the increased happiness and connection you will experience as you notice judgments and transform them into a more compassionate understanding of needs. For me, it has helped create a deeper sense of meaning and purpose and a deeper connection with everyone in my life – from a thirty-second relationship in an elevator to a life-long relationship with my parents.

IN PRACTICE

WHAT ARE WE LISTENING FOR?

*How Listening for the Needs inside Your Judgments
Can Change Your Life, and Someone Else's*

Three people stood before a classic Monet canvas. One noticed the cypress trees drifting into invisibility. Another noticed the calm character of the water. The third noticed a chip on the side of the frame. It has become clear to me that we have the power to choose what we see and what we listen for. And by so doing, we can change the very nature of our experience. I have learned I can listen for thoughts, ideas, opinions or judgments, or I can listen for life-energy (feelings and underlying needs and values).

LISTENING TO JUDGMENTS AND THOUGHTS

The other evening, at the dinner table, my friend Brian was saying how our other friend Frankie was "flaky" and "too impulsive". Since I did not agree with Brian's assessment, I was a little agitated, and my first thought was, "Wow, what a judgmental attitude. He's projecting all his stuff on Frankie." Luckily, I did not say these words. Instead, I noticed that I thought them and also noticed that I was feeling agitated.

I say luckily because I don't imagine it would have gone well if I stayed with my judgment thought. Two signals: one, my judgment thought, "He was being judgmental", and two, my agitation let me know I was disconnecting. Checking in with myself, I realized I wanted more connection and understanding. I figured I was not likely to get it by listening to his thoughts and judgments or my assessment of them. By doing that, I would likely disconnect further.

LISTENING FOR FEELINGS AND NEEDS

Because of my intention to experience more compassion, I have developed an alternative for myself. Through *empathic listening* I can listen for needs and make them the focus of my interactions.

Because of my presence and focus on needs, the conversation turned toward other things, like how Brian just didn't understand why Frankie did what he did. As we talked, it became clearer that Brian wanted more connection, clarity and, as it turned out, inclusion. The conversation began to slow and our thoughts, ideas, and judgments gave way to our awareness of needs for clarity, connection and inclusion.

Talking about these things felt so much better than talking about how "flaky" or "impulsive" or "judgmental" someone is. And when the needs, not the judgments, were in our awareness, we could connect deeply about things we valued in our lives - even think of ways to address those needs through requests – a completely different and wonderful experience, to be sure.

It might not seem like that big of a deal, yet in that split second of noticing my judgments and being able to shift my focus to needs, everything changed, and life got more wonderful.

PRACTICES

PRACTICE 1

Noticing and Translating Judgments in Others - Keep a small journal with you throughout the day. Make 1 to 5 entries per day that include judgment words spoken by someone. Later on, when you have time, sit down with the Needs List and see if you can figure out what need was unmet in the other person. Remember, it's VERY helpful to limit the words you use to those on the list.

PRACTICE 2

Noticing and Translating Judgments in Oneself – Keep a small journal with you throughout the day. Make 1 to 5 entries per day that include judgment words you said or were thinking of saying. Later on, when you have time, sit down with the Needs List and see if you can figure out what need of yours the judgment was about. Remember, it's VERY helpful to limit the words you use to those on the list

PRACTICE 3

Judgment Liberation – Think of someone you have held a judgment about for a long time (more than twelve weeks). See if you can figure out what need of yours has you thinking this way. Then, think of 3 other ways you could meet this need.

CHAPTER 3

THE CONCEPT

WE ARE ALL EQUIPPED WITH ON-BOARD NEED RADAR

In previous chapters, we have explored the idea of looking at all acts as an attempt to meet needs. We've also worked on noticing and translating our judgments as a way of finding out about needs. Although doing this may be challenging at first, when we can bring our consciousness to needs, we are more able to be compassionate.

There is yet another way to bring our awareness to needs. This way is called feeling - quite simply, feeling. I have come to realize that when I am aware of how I'm feeling, I can track how well my needs are met or not. This is based on the simple concept that:

> *When our needs are met, we feel fulfilled and satisfied...*
> *happy even... we feel good – and when our needs are*
> *not met, we feel unfulfilled, unsatisfied, unhappy... we*
> *feel bad.*

Think about it. If I gave you a thousand dollars (no strings attached), I'm guessing you would feel pretty good (needs met). On the other hand, if someone somehow took a thousand dollars from you, I suspect you would not feel so great (needs unmet). This relationship between feelings and needs means that if we can be aware of our feelings, they will provide *guidance*. They will inform us about the "metness" of our needs.

We can notice this over and over. Eat a delicious, healthy meal... feel good, needs met. Don't eat for a day... you feel hungry, not-good, needs not met. A friend sends you a little card, thanking you for being their friend... usually, that feels pretty good, needs met. If someone starts a lawsuit against you... not so good, needs not met.

WE CAN LOOK AT EVERY FEELING THIS WAY

By noticing feelings and connecting them to needs, we start to see things differently. I call it "the parallel universe of feelings and needs". Seeing this universe, by noticing our feelings, gives us a greater ability to consider our own (or someone else's) needs... and that means more compassion.

That said, I feel compelled to share that for me, this skill of feeling (or noticing) feelings, naming feelings and connecting them to needs is a lifework. Although the ideas discussed here are relatively simple and easy to understand, actually putting them into practice can be very challenging. The practices in this chapter address this.

THE GOOD NEWS AND BAD NEWS ABOUT FEELINGS

First, the bad news: Most of us are challenged to notice or feel our feelings. Many of us have come to believe they don't exist. Some of us have come to the conclusion that we're better off without them.

The good news: They're still here. As far as I have seen, no one with a living human body/mind can stop having feelings. We just learn to stop noticing them. Simply put, this means one of the most important skills that we can develop to have more compassion in our lives

15

is the skill of feeling feelings. This empowers us to connect to needs, which in turn, engenders compassion.

IN PRACTICE

My First Day of School and What I Learned about Feelings and Needs

I will never forget my first day of school and what I learned that day.

I remember standing at the bus stop in the early morning chill of the fall. I was with my mother, feeling really anxious and confused – not really understanding what was going on. When the bus arrived, my mother informed me that I was to get on the bus. In that moment, my whole world changed. I became awash in fear. I knew clearly how much I did *not* want to go. I did *not* want to be on a bus with strangers or go to a big strange building full of more strangers. I wanted to stay home in my house with my toys and my mother. That morning, not a cell in my body wanted to go to school. I was terrified.

I refused to get on the bus. Clinging to my mother, crying, I begged to be allowed to stay home. As all this was going on, the bus driver stepped down from his driver's seat and walked over to my mother and me. He then nonchalantly pulled me from my mother, threw me over his shoulder and carried me onto the bus as I screamed, begging and pleading not to go. Maybe I'm mistaken, but it seemed like he had done this before. As the bus pulled away with me pounding my little fists on the inevitably closed steel and glass door, I was learning something.

As upset as I was, it didn't matter. My feelings, as strong as they were, didn't matter. I was going to school that day.

I learned that feeling my feelings and being aware of my needs can be a horrible experience. I learned that I could experience tremendous pain and desire, and there was really not much that I could do about it. For me that day, and for many of us still, feelings and needs have mainly been nothing but a source of pain - bad news that we don't want to receive. Some of us have learned to ignore, disregard, or deny the existence of them. For some, it helps us survive.

I'm sharing this, not to blame my mother or the teacher, or the bus driver, or society. I'm certainly not saying anything was *wrong*. I'm sharing this experience with you because remembering it helps me understand my relationship to feelings. I'm hoping it might help you understand yours. In the practice of compassion, feelings play a large role. Often the path to compassion starts at noticing feelings, feeling them, understanding them, and communicating clearly about them. So when it comes to feelings, this memory of my first day of school helps me to see how I'm trained or *untrained*.

HUNGER

As children and often as adults, we eat by the clock – hence the term "lunchtime". In school, we generally ate at noon, not when we felt hungry.

Additionally, many of us have heard the phrase "finish your plate" or have been encouraged in one form or another to eat all the food we have been served – *not* to eat until we feel full.

SLEEP

As children and often as adults we sleep by the clock – hence the invention and widespread use of the alarm clock. As children, most of us had "bedtimes" that had more to do with what time it was than being tired.

Eating and sleeping are crucial human functions, yet many of us do them without an awareness of what our body tells us about them. So now, when I look back on my upbringing, it helps me understand why I distanced myself from my feelings. It seemed they weren't really serving any purpose. To a large extent, I learned to ignore them.

As an adult, I have discovered a reason to feel my feelings, to pay attention to them. Now, they tell me about my needs, my life. Now my feelings are guidance. And the more I bring my awareness to them, the more self-connection I can have. The more I feel my feelings, the more I understand how I am – how my needs are, or are not, being met.

In my years as a trainer and "empathologist", I have come to believe that we all have a "feeling feelings muscle" that we can develop – all of us. And when we develop that skill (muscle) and create a deeper relationship with our feelings, it gives them a new purpose and meaning.

It has been my repeated experience that when we have a deeper relationship with feelings (and needs), almost all of us experience more self-connection and connection with others. That, in turn, engenders compassion, both inward and outward.

I find it important to remember that first day of school and what I learned that day. It gives me more compassion for my current-day "grown-up self" when I have difficulty experiencing or understanding feelings. And that helps me stay with my practice – and then inevitably, life becomes more wonderful.

PRACTICES

Note: The practices below are designed to get us into the habit of even thinking about feelings throughout our day. Remembering to think this way is a challenge unto itself,

*so journaling as described below, helps us remember to
turn our awareness to feelings (and eventually needs).
Having a physical journal acts as a reminder.*

*I remember the first time I did these practices I kept
getting frustrated because I would carry this journal
around with me all day and not use it. It was this very
frustration that helped me see how much I wanted to
have growth and integration. It took a while, but my
frustration guided me to eventually do my practice and
actually use the journal. Pretty cool.*

PRACTICE 1

Notice Feelings – Keep a journal with you throughout the day. This
can be a small notebook or even a folded piece of paper. Make 2 to 4
entries per day that include something that someone else did or said
and the feeling (or feelings) you experienced at that moment.

Later on, when you have time, sit down with the Feelings List and
see if you can find a similar feeling word from the list that describes
how you were feeling. Give the list a thorough looking over. See if
there are other words that reflect your experience as well.

Then, look at the Needs List and see if you can figure out what need
or needs your feeling was about. Remember, it's VERY helpful to
limit the words you use to those on the list.

PRACTICE 2

Notice More Feelings – Keep a small journal with you throughout
the day. Make 2 to 4 entries per day that include something you
did, said or were thinking of saying and the feeling (or feelings) you
experienced at that moment. Again, later on, when you have time,

sit down with the Feelings List and see if you can find feeling words from the list that describe how you were feeling. Again, give the list a thorough looking over. See if there are other words that reflect your experience as well.

Then look at the Needs List and see if you can figure out what need or needs your feeling was about. Remember, here too, it's VERY important to limit the words you use to those on the list.

CHAPTER 4

THE CONCEPT

WHAT'S THE BIG DEAL WITH NEEDS?

When I was first developing my practice of compassion, I was amazed at how connected and compassionate I could be when living in the awareness of needs. It was a bit of a shock, really.

My practice of noticing needs gives me a way to see any other person as someone who is *just like me*. Perhaps they're acting differently than I would choose to act. Perhaps they're doing something I don't like. Yet ultimately, when I'm in "needs consciousness" I can find my way to a more compassionate view.

In my experience, when I am in this *state* or *field* of "compassionate understanding", I can dislike, even abhor someone's actions, without experiencing judgment or hatred toward them, as a person.

So one of the things we can do to create a more compassionate existence is to practice seeing needs. Many of us have already had this experience in our practices from Chapters 1 to 3. It's a skill we will continue to develop throughout the book.

We can think of our awareness of needs as a foothold for compassion. As we develop our awareness, the foothold grows to a perch, to a resting place, to a field.

In this chapter, I would like to share some ways to think about needs that have changed my life in wonderful ways.

> *Note: I imagine it would be VERY helpful to have a Needs List in front of you as you read this.*

What Are Needs Really?

As I said earlier, I was amazed at this whole *need* thing. So I pondered, trying to really wrap my head around what needs are and what function they have. I asked myself, "What do you call someone that has no needs?" My answer surprised me. "Dead." Think about it. Any living creature has needs. No needs – no life.

Pondering further, I asked, "Then what does that make needs?" My next answer was surprising still – they are the impulses of life. They are the gift of life. They are how we conceive of this thing we are all going through called life."

I imagine that is one of the reasons it is so profoundly connecting when we relate to ourselves and others through our feelings and needs – we are relating to life.

Needs As Being Universal

Needs are a thing we all have in common, as humans in particular – we are all having a human life. As I look at the Needs List, I can see that every need on there I have had met and would like to have met more. I suspect that is true for every one of us. Needs are universal – no matter what age, gender, culture, spiritual orientation or anything else we are.

Aren't There Good and Bad Needs?

Many people wonder about needs versus wants, versus things we would love to have, etc. I often hear the words "inappropriate needs", or "irresponsible needs".

I have noticed that thinking in that way tends to disconnect us from needs and ultimately each other. If you're looking to *be right* or to influence someone's behavior, seeing needs this way could serve you quite well. However, if you're looking to experience more compassion, understanding, and connection, it probably won't help.

Needs Are Not Strategies

When we distinguish needs from the ways we try to fulfill them (strategies), we have more opportunities to engage in compassionate thinking and action.

My understanding of this difference between needs and strategies changes the way I see every conflict and in fact, every human act.

Here's a practice that may help you understand the difference. If you look on your Needs List, you will probably have a hard time finding the word "job" on there or "house" or "spouse". Now take a moment and see if you can find the needs on the list that are met by having a house or a job or a spouse. Cool, right?

Needs Don't Conflict, Strategies Do

When I focus on needs, instead of the strategies I might engage in to fulfill them, I can see things that I simply couldn't see before.

You could say that when we are in "strategy mode", we only have two choices, do the strategy or not. When we are in "need mode", we have *ten thousand* strategies available to us to meet any need (metaphorically speaking, of course).

IN PRACTICE

THE RIDDLE OF MR. AND MRS. SMITH

Mr. Smith and Mrs. Smith are getting home from work at the same time. As they walk in, Mr. Smith turns to Mrs. Smith and with his eyes half closed, says in a waning voice, "Honey, I just had the worst day at work, and I need some space."

Hearing this, Mrs. Smith moves toward her exhausted spouse. She wraps her arms around his limp arms and torso, rests her head on his shoulder and says. "Honey, that's so weird, because I just had the worst day of work ever and I need some company. I gotta talk about this."

Do their needs conflict?

Wait!

Before you answer, try this:

1) Write down what you think their respective needs are from the Needs List – his and hers (see Appendix B).

2) Then, write down 3 ways they could each get those needs met – 3 for him, 3 for her. It helps to use your imagination a bit here.

The more I do this, the more I am able to take the perspective that their needs are *not* in conflict. It's the *strategy* of having one another contribute to their needs – at this time – that could be seen as the conflict.

Over and over again, I have witnessed, when we can see this distinction between *needs* and *strategies* we become empowered to think of many more ways to get our needs considered and addressed. It also empowers us to do the same for others. This is big stuff.

PRACTICES

PRACTICE 1

Read the Needs List (see Appendix B) – Notice what comes up in you as you do this.

PRACTICE 2

Print a copy of the Needs List (see Appendix B) – Then, along the left side of each need word, write down a rating on a scale of 1 to 10 in terms of how well it is met in your life (1 = hardly met at all and 10 = very met).

PRACTICE 3

Noticing Needs – Renew your practice from Chapter 1 – Keep a small journal with you throughout the day. Make 1 to 5 entries per day that include an act or words spoken by someone, and what need(s) you imagine they were trying to meet. Remember, it's *very* helpful to limit the words you use to those on the Needs List.

PRACTICE 4

Needs Liberation – Think of someone that you think is preventing you from getting a need met. Write down the need from the Needs List. Then, think of 3 ways you could get this need met *without* that person. It helps to use your imagination a bit here too.

CHAPTER 5

THE CONCEPT

EMPATHY, THE BREATH OF COMPASSION

In previous chapters, we have focused on increasing our experience of compassion. The basic operating premise has been that when we can get to an awareness of needs, we are more able to access compassion.

The two paths to this awareness that we have worked with are:

1) Noticing and translating judgments into needs

2) Noticing feelings and connecting them to needs (met or unmet)

The practice of identifying feelings and needs works inwardly and outwardly. It is the practice of self-empathy and empathy – stopping, noticing feelings and needs inwardly (in us), and outwardly (in others) – that is the breath of compassion. In […] Out […]

From here on throughout the book, we will be distinguishing, developing, and refining ways to master the skills of empathy, and accessing more compassion.

As we increase our skills and awareness, the very experience of our daily lives will begin to change. It will inevitably include more connection, compassion, and joy.

The practices for this chapter include an exercise called "Shifting Toward Compassion". This exercise guides us through the fundamental acts of self-empathy and empathy. It is a process we will build on, most likely, for the rest of our lives.

We may find that there are obstacles keeping us from moving deeper into this practice, and we will work with those too.

For now, I would like to celebrate that we are even talking about these things we call empathy and self-empathy.

IN PRACTICE

THE BOND BOYS FIND HARMONY

A few years back, Harpo, our dog of fourteen years, was seriously ill, and it didn't appear that he would be with us much longer.

My son Pat was visiting to spend some time before Harpo left us. We took Harpo to the veterinarian's office together. Dr. Newhouse let us know that the best thing we could do was make our little family member comfortable, and that Harpo himself would let us know when he was ready to go.

Throughout the day, Pat was being what I was characterizing as "grumpy" or angry. Going through my own grief around Harpo's condition was now compounded by being with an "angry person".

After we returned home, Patrick created a list of things to do to make Harpo more comfortable. When he told me about this, I was quite hesitant (if not flat-out unwilling) to implement his plan. In my mind, I had already done everything necessary to provide for Harpo's comfort. It seemed to me that Pat's ideas would be of no real use. Pat and I were at odds – disconnected. I found myself having a very unpleasant experience.

Then I checked in with myself. "What was this? Why am I so out of sorts? Why do I feel so unhappy right now? What's missing?" I realized I was yearning to have more harmony, more connection. Then, I wondered what I might do to have that. I realized I could wonder about Pat's feelings and needs too.

I guessed that he was experiencing a deep and profound pain about his little friend – in fact, a childhood friend – dying. I imagined he was feeling angry, scared, anxious and helpless, watching this happen and ultimately unable to do anything to stop it.

From this awareness, I had a shift. I saw that Pat's list was not completely about Harpo. It was a way for Patrick to take care of himself, to help him stay centered, to act on his sense of helplessness, to ease his pain. With that awareness, there was nothing I wanted to do more than join Patrick in his "to-do" list for Harpo.

From that moment on, it was a very different experience.

Harpo had a natural affinity for connection. He would actually run in circles of glee when he saw people hugging. It wasn't long before he came to join us.

PRACTICES

PRACTICE 1

Review – Review the "Shifting Toward Compassion" exercise once or twice or more times (see Appendix C).

PRACTICE 2

Increasing Awareness – Keep a small journal with you throughout the day. Make 1 to 5 entries per day that include the description of an action done or words spoken by someone (yourself included) and what feelings and what needs were present in that moment.

For this particular exercise, choose *uneventful* moments, *not* a moment of upset. Look for more subtle occurrences: someone calling to their child, someone saying "excuse me", you saying "thank you" to someone, and so on.

Many of us wait until we're "hit over the head" with a situation before we start our practice of awareness. This practice helps us increase our awareness of feelings and needs by proactively noticing them in more subtle situations.

This practice also helps us see that these energies (feelings and needs) are everywhere.

CHAPTER 6

THE CONCEPT

HIDDEN JUDGMENTS

At this point in the book, you may have developed the skill of translating judgments into needs (or are beginning to – I get it, it can be challenging). This will be a recurring and vital practice in our journey to having more compassion in our lives.

So it follows that the more we have the skill of identifying judgments, the more opportunity we have to increase our awareness of needs and therefore, our experience of compassion.

In this chapter I would like to share two ways that we can increase our compassion by noticing our "hidden judgments":

1) Distinguishing *observations* from *judgments*

2) Noticing "non-feeling words"

DISTINGUISHING OBSERVATIONS FROM JUDGMENTS

I can handle your telling me
What I did or didn't do.
And I can handle your interpretations,
But please don't mix the two.

If you want to confuse any issue,
I can tell you how to do it:

Mix together what I do
With how you react to it.

Tell me you're disappointed
With the unfinished chores you see,
But calling me "irresponsible"
Is no way to motivate me.

And tell me you're feeling hurt
When I say "no" to your advances,
But calling me frigid
Won't increase your future chances.

Yes, I can handle your telling me
What I did or didn't do,
And I can handle your interpretations,
But please don't mix the two.

— Marshall Rosenberg,
Friend, Mentor, Teacher, Poet

As we have discussed in earlier chapters, it can be disconnecting to speak in terms of judgment, yet most of us struggle to fully notice our judgments. By learning to recognize and speak in ways that include more observation and less judgment, we can increase the amount of connection we are likely to experience when we are talking to others (and ourselves).

In the practices section of this chapter, there is an exercise that helps us distinguish these two modes of communicating (judging versus observing). This, in turn, gives us more choice about how we speak and what we experience as a result. FYI, this exercise can be a challenging endeavor.

DISTINGUISHING NON-FEELING WORDS

"Non-feeling words" are words that we use as if they are feelings, although they are not really feelings. In fact, they can be seen as judgments disguised in "feeling language". Although we have touched on this topic in earlier chapters, it can take some real intention to develop our ability to notice and translate "non-feeling words" and the thoughts that go with them.

For example, I may say, "I feel abandoned." Although, if you think about it, "abandoned" is something that happens (or happened). It is not *actually* a feeling.

That said, it doesn't mean that if someone says they're "feeling abandoned", that they are not having feelings (or needs). It just means they are not included in the words (and likely consciousness).

By translating (or connecting) these words to the feelings and needs "inside" them, we can experience more connection, understanding and compassion. For example, in the case of "abandoned", I can imagine that the person saying that, feels lonely or scared and would like to have more connection, companionship, trust or love. When I think about these feelings and needs (and not the word "abandoned"), I am more likely to experience connection and a more compassionate understanding of what they are going through.

> *Note: Many of us, when we become aware of "non-feeling words", are tempted to "correct" people who use them. We may even say things like "That's not a feeling!" As it turns out, that rarely ends up being a connecting experience. I have learned (the hard way) to simply translate or unpack "non-feeling" words inside my own head to create my own sense of compassionate understanding.*

I have found this practice of seeing the feelings and needs inside "non-feeling words" to be particularly powerful (even transformational) when I notice and translate my own use of these words.

In the practices section this chapter, there is an exercise that helps us learn the *unpacking* process when it comes to some of these words.

IN PRACTICE

THIS WINE IS TERRIBLE!

I was sitting with some friends after a practice group one evening, sipping some wine I had just acquired. When I took my first taste, I was shocked by the intense, almost overwhelming flavors I encountered. Finishing my sip, I exclaimed, "This wine is terrible!"

As I looked around the table, I saw expressions of surprise and dismay on the faces of my friends. After a moment, it occurred to me that they were enjoying their glasses of wine.

I spoke again. "I mean, this wine is too intense for me." The looks shifted from dismay to understanding and our conversation instantly returned to a more connected state.

In that moment, we went from being three people having a disconnect over "the truth" about this wine, to three people drinking wine that one of us didn't really like.

Granted, this was just a little moment in time, one that may or may not have had any serious consequence. Although, I will never forget the way those two different sentences subtly, yet clearly, changed our experience.

PRACTICES

PRACTICE 1

"Shifting Toward Compassion" – Continue working with this exercise (see Appendix C) – This time, start using observations in addition to quotes, such as actions. You can also work with your own judgment thoughts by writing the words "I'm telling myself _____." For example, "I'm telling myself Chris is selfish."

PRACTICE 2

Experiencing Judgments versus Needs – Write down 4 judgments you have about your own needs. For example, "I don't deserve to have them", "they are a sign of weakness" – take your time.

Next, choose your top 5 favorite needs (things that you would really love to experience) from the Needs List and write them down. Scan and ponder your lists. Notice how you feel as you "take-in" these two different lists.

PRACTICE 3

Non-Feeling Word Game – This simple game is a practice in finding "hidden judgments" and *unpacking* the feelings and needs inside them (see Appendix D).

PRACTICE 4

Heavier Lifting – Distinguishing Evaluations and Judgments – This exercise helps us find the "hidden judgments" inside our words. It is also practice in speaking in a "judgment-free" manner (see Appendix E).

CHAPTER 7

THE CONCEPT

MORE ABOUT FEELINGS

Since Chapter 3, we have focused on the skill of noticing feelings and connecting them to needs (again, at least we are beginning to – this stuff takes time). Again, this is a recurring and vital practice in our journey to having more compassion in our lives.

As we develop this skill of connecting feelings to needs, we will inevitably have more awareness of needs and therefore, our experience of compassion will increase.

Many of us have learned to have a different relationship to our feelings. Instead of noticing – if not welcoming – our feelings as guidance, we stay separated from them. This separation can take many forms.

JUDGING OUR FEELINGS

Most of us have heard (or thought) the words, "You shouldn't feel that way", or "I don't have the right to feel this way." These thoughts put us *at odds* with our feelings and make us less likely to want to feel them.

FEARING OUR FEELINGS

Many of us have a fearful relationship with our feelings. We see them as a source of pain – things to be avoided. With practice, we can learn to see our feelings as a guide to the source of our pain (instead of seeing them *as the source* of our pain).

As our practice of welcoming and feeling our feelings increases, we can deepen our relationship to them, as well as the needs they are telling us about. This increases our capacity for compassion and ultimately, for making life more wonderful.

IGNORING OUR FEELINGS

Some of us have learned to ignore or suppress our feelings. We have grown up hearing words like "Grow up!" or "Don't be such a cry baby". We have been encouraged, if not commanded, to cut ourselves off from our feelings.

I recall, as a young boy playing football in the fourth grade, tackling my classmate Gerard. Gerard weighed about a hundred and fifty pounds to my eighty. When I tackled him, he fell on my head, just off the sideline. The sideline was made of blacktop.

I remember the excruciating pain of Gerard's weight pressing and scraping my ear and cheek into the pavement. I also remember excusing myself and heading home. I walked with my back to my friends, waiting until I was out of earshot so I could start crying. The pressure to "man up" was astounding and oppressive for my little body/mind, but I did it. I learned to push my feelings down.

As I have asked around, I've learned that most of us have had experiences like that.

FEELINGS AS MESSENGERS

These days, I find it way more useful to see feelings as messengers – little beings inside me that are helping me to navigate my life. They tell me, moment by moment, how I am and what I would like more of (or less of) right now.

It is this relationship with my feelings that helps me stay more connected to myself, to life, and ultimately, to the life-energy of those around me.

In my experience, these messengers are my dear, devoted friends – so much so, that they often refuse to leave until I fully receive the message they have for me.

The practices in this chapter will help us discover, renew, and deepen our relationship to the life-energy we call feelings and eventually help us to deepen our experience of compassion and to create a more wonderful life.

IN PRACTICE

SPILLED PAPERS AND THIRTY SECONDS OF SELF-EMPATHY

One of the things I appreciate most about seeing my feelings as guidance is that it almost always brings me to me – my center, my experience and, ultimately, my compassion.

I remember, one Sunday afternoon, I was straightening up my apartment when I came across a small pile of papers my partner had left on the bed. As I gently pulled the bedspread to straighten it beneath the pile, the pile shifted and the papers poured into a heap between the bed and the wall. As I reached for them, they proceeded to splay under the bed, through the dust and who knows what else (yuck!). Within a few seconds, I had a big, unreachable mess to deal with.

I noticed anger at my partner welling up in me. Luckily, it occurred to me that something was going on for me. I took a breath and checked in with myself.

By turning my attention to my feelings, I was able to see that I was frustrated and really just wanted some order and ease. I was also angry, blaming my partner for the mess, thinking "She *shouldn't* have left those papers on the bed."

By checking in with myself, I created a new choice for myself. I could go with the judgment that she *should* be more organized – or tune into my needs. I decided to focus on my need for order and simply reach under the bed and clean up the papers. As I did this, blaming became less important. Actually, the whole thing was kind of a freak accident and it almost seemed funny by then. By that time, it seemed that nobody had done anything "wrong".

Just as I was having this shift inside me, I heard my partner's voice from the living room, "Are you OK in there?"

"Yes," I said. I was.

As I called out my simple reply, I realized that if I had heard that same question only thirty seconds earlier, I would have still been in the "blaming place". From that place, I would have likely said something that wouldn't have matched my values and almost certainly would have contributed to an instant disconnection.

I'm grateful for the choice I gave myself in those moments. By turning inward, with a curiosity about my feelings and my needs (instead of my judgment), I was able to transform the moment back to a place of connection and compassion – for me, and for her. Sweet.

PRACTICES

PRACTICE 1

Me and My Feelings – Think of a situation in your life where you experience a high level of stimulation or pain. Notice the feeling. Feel the feeling. Stay with this feeling for a minute or so, simply noticing and feeling your feeling. Stay with it.

You may notice you are judging, avoiding or backing away from this feeling. Notice when this happens. Then go back to feeling your feeling. Repeat. Try this for 2 to 5 minutes.

> *Note: This exercise is an effective way to find the thoughts and reactions you have in relation to your feelings. By doing this, you will create the opportunity to have a deeper relationship with your feelings (and yourself) over time. For now, just notice what happens.*

PRACTICE 2

Deeper Exploration – Noticing What I Tell Myself about Feelings – Write down 4 judgments you have about your feelings (ex. "I don't deserve to have them", "they are going to hurt me", and so on).

> *Hint: You will usually discover some of these in Practice 1.*

Next, write down what need(s) you are meeting, or attempting to meet, by holding these judgments.

After that, write down what need(s) you are *not* meeting by holding these judgments. Notice anything?

CHAPTER 8

THE CONCEPT

THE WISDOM INSIDE THE JUDGMENT

We can think of ourselves as having two different ways of thinking to choose from: the first, to pursue our judgmental or *habitual* thought patterns or, the second, to pursue an awareness of feelings and needs (life-energy).

Ironically, many of us think of these choices as "good" and "bad" –feelings and needs awareness as "good" (we *should* be in this awareness) and judgment as "bad" (we *shouldn't* be in judgment). I say ironically, because these thoughts are a form of judgment thinking (i.e. good/bad).

As we have discussed previously, judgments hold inside them a path to discovering needs. So, when we hold our judgments as being "bad", we can inadvertently disconnect ourselves from our needs. In effect, we stop our process before it starts. The two scenarios below illustrate my point and the potential pitfalls and opportunities that await us.

SCENARIO ONE

I find myself thinking that a coworker is "inconsiderate". If I think I'm doing something "wrong" by thinking this way, I will likely stop myself at "inconsiderate" (thinking, "I *shouldn't* think this way").

As we have practiced before, I now have the opportunity to translate "inconsiderate" into my desire to experience, perhaps, more consideration, or care – and with that, I have a connection to my needs (life-energy)…

But wait!

Scenario Two

I find myself thinking that a coworker is "inconsiderate". This time I think, "Good news, my life-energy is calling me. Let's explore." So I let my judgments run, knowing that my judgments are not coming from an understanding of my life-energy in a connected way. Why? Because I *also* know, that although they are expressing my life-energy in a *disconnected* way, I can *translate* that into a more compassionate and connected experience.

So I let it flow – "Yeah, she's 'inconsiderate' and a 'big liar' – and she's 'a user'!"

Now I have three ways I can find out about my life-energy. So as we have practiced before, I now have the opportunity to translate. This time I have three times as much to work with, translate and ultimately connect about.

I have "inconsiderate", "liar", and "user". Now I can tap into my desire to experience more consideration and care – and now perhaps trust, self-care, mutuality and more – a deeper, more complete, connection to my life-energy.

This process of letting my judgments run (in my mind) can be seen as enjoying "the judgment show". I like this phrase because it creates a distinction between two parts of me, my life-connected part and my not-so-life-connected part. I can watch my judgments as preliminary information, not as "the truth". And ultimately, I can have a more complete connection, more understanding and more compassion.

This "two-headed" approach takes some time and practice, although the benefits are growth provoking and profound.

IN PRACTICE

STRANDED

Some time ago, I was part of a training team for a four-day intensive training. One of the trainers was a person I had never worked with before.

As the training progressed, I noticed I was getting agitated and annoyed as I watched and worked with this trainer. He said several things that did not match my understanding of the practice of compassion. He also said some things that I strongly believed stimulated pain, mistrust, and misunderstanding among the participants.

By the second day of the training, I was in knots. Although I was trying desperately to make observations (and to some degree succeeding), I still felt horrible. I was distracted, annoyed, and generally off my center. Something was missing. It seemed I was dead-ended.

Normally in these situations I would call my empathy buddy. In this particular situation, since I had no phone service, I had no ability to contact her. It would be up to me to go deeper on my own.

I decided to write a "Judgment Journal". It looked something like this:

JUDGMENT THOUGHT	NEEDS OR VALUES
He cares more about having "guru" status than contributing to people	Care, competence, self-aware-ness, contribution
He's "sabotaging" our training	Partnership, support, shared reality
He's "irresponsible"	Care, competence, contribu-tion, learning, growth
He's an "egomaniac"	Awareness, presence, mutual-ity, community, partnership

As I wrote and read my words, I could more clearly see the life-energy that was moving inside me. With this awareness, I could more readily have a dialog about things I value and strive to experience, things that I love. When I could see my *habitual thinking* right next to my *needs and values thinking*, I created more clarity and choice as to what I believed would serve us best.

I had a dialog with the other trainer. It was a difficult conversation – and yet, by sharing my needs, not my judgments, we could connect, understand, and cooperate more readily. It was difficult – not impossible.

In the end, it was my judgments that gave me the opportunity to find my needs and values. This in turn allowed me to live in a more connected and compassionate place.

PRACTICES

PRACTICE 1

Start a Judgment Journal – In a journal, write down judgments that you find yourself holding about someone (including yourself).

Later on, when you have time, sit down and write all the judgments you can think of about this person (yes, even if it's you). Have a good go at it. Be specific. Not just that they are a "jerk". What kind of "jerk". A "self-centered jerk"? A "lazy jerk"? The more specific our judgments, the more information we can get about our needs. Weird, but it works.

Then look at the Needs List and see if you can figure out what needs your different judgments are telling you about.

CHAPTER 9

THE CONCEPT

WHY IS THIS SO BLEEPING HARD?

My Being and My Robot

When I first started studying compassionate consciousness, I was amazed at how simple it was. This was immediately followed by my amazement of how difficult it was. How could something so simple be so hard? The answer to this question didn't necessarily make my journey to a more compassionate life any easier. However, it did allow me to be easier on myself. Below is a little poem I wrote that puts it into perspective:

> I have a little robot
> That goes around with me.
> Sometimes it's thinking what
> I'm thinking,
> Sometimes it's thinking me.

This little poem helps me to think of myself as having two parts: my "being" and my "robot". My "being" has no habitual thoughts. It is always present and conscious. However, my "being" lives with my "robot", my human body and brain. My "robot" is more habitual in thought, language and action. Although my "robot" does change its habits, it does it a great deal slower than I would like. The good news is that it does eventually come around if I persist. This is where practice comes in.

For example, when I was first studying, I wanted to think about needs more often (mine and others), particularly in difficult situations. My "being" knew this would bring more connection and understanding, and ultimately, be more life-serving for me and those around me. Yet my "robot" continued to think about blame – how other people were *responsible,* or what people *should* or *shouldn't* do or say (including myself).

My inability to follow my own intention to be more compassionate was disturbing and puzzling to me. My "robot" or "habitual self" was holding my "being" back. Why did this happen?

As it turns out, there is a very good explanation. The more our brain's synapses connect in a certain pattern, the more they tend to reconnect in the exact same pattern. It's this very characteristic that allows us to learn and remember things. So we can think of many thoughts as *habits.* This is why we don't have to think very hard when brushing our teeth or getting off at our bus stop. We are thinking *habitually.* Our "robot" is doing its job without us.

Over time, habitual patterns can grow to be much more sophisticated than tooth brushing. They influence everything we do and think, from choosing what to eat, to thinking our boss is a pain in the neck. Habitual thoughts particularly affect how we relate to ourselves, our families, and others close to us. Sounding familiar?

In some cases our "robot" makes life easier. It allows us to multi-task and can even protect us from danger. And yet there are other cases where we can find ourselves at odds with it, like when we are trying out new thoughts or behaviors, or like when we are trying to integrate more compassionate thought patterns.

Although our "robot" influences the rate at which our thoughts and behaviors will shift, ultimately, with intention and practice, our "being" can help create new habits over time. Our "being" can be thought of as a *creative force* or *programmer* that can, with practice and repetition, ultimately determine our direction and experience. It is our "being" that can bring new awareness to every moment. It is our "being" that brings our "robot" to read <u>The Compassion Book</u>, our "being" that brings us to the gym and feeds us healthier food.

When I think of my thoughts and actions from this perspective of "robot" and "being", I feel less anxious about the rate of progress in my integration. I can be more compassionate, understanding and present to myself in any new learning. That makes my process less painful and more rewarding, and I'm able to stick with it. When I stick with it, slowly and surely, my "being" and my "robot" become more aligned.

This is why practice and repetition are so powerful as ways to integrate compassion into our lives.

The way I see it, there's plenty of support for my "robot" self (habitual), so I make a special effort to support my "being" (conscious) self.

IN PRACTICE

TWO ME'S

One afternoon, I was helping my son Collin with a sustainable energy project he was working on (my chosen profession before I became a trainer and writer). We were discussing various options that were available when I noticed we were practically yelling at each other.

I was surprised and confused, wondering, "Who is this person (me) who is speaking in such a rapid, staccato fashion – hardly waiting for a response, not listening, only promoting my ideas?"

As I thought about this, I realized it was time to *slow down*. I asked Collin to just bear with me for a moment while I figured out what was happening.

After some moments of self-inquiry, I realized that two parts of my "robot" had come to visit.

The first was the *father* part (of the past) that used his power to "over-rule" his son – taking the authority he had raised his children with for years (before my training reconnected me to my compassion).

The second part was the *business* part, that had been trained to "get the job done, and get it done now", the part that I had programmed to survive and prosper in a world of competitive business.

I realized that these two parts of my "robot" had gotten together and taken over the conversation, leaving my compassionate "being" in silence... almost.

I used this awareness to shift my experience. I took a breath, took another breath, looked at Collin and said, "Collin, I don't want to talk like this. Let's start again." And we did.

My "robot" subsided, and I listened, considered, and spoke with Collin from my more compassionate "being". It was a very different and wonderful conversation. I listened, I learned, and I loved our connection – and we got the job done in a way that was in harmony with my desire to live a more compassionate life.

That afternoon, it became so clear to me how much vigilance, self-awareness, and self-connection it takes to live in a more con-nected state, even after years of study and practice. The good news that day – it was possible.

PRACTICES

PRACTICE 1

Noticing Disconnecting Habitual Thoughts – Find a word or expression that you use every day that may disconnect you from your conscious self. For example, "have to", as in "I *have to* go to the store" or "I *have to* do the laundry". Try to notice yourself using those words and then try replacing them with words that more accurately reflect a deeper connection, or that more accurately reflect what is happening in you – like "I am choosing to go to the store" or "I'm going to do the laundry".

Perhaps there are other words such as "like" or "really" or "actually" that you use out of habit that, when you think about it, don't contribute to your message or express what's going on for you. See if you can find another set of words – or maybe fewer words – that will accomplish your communication in a more conscious way. Warning – this can be quite difficult. Keep trying!

PRACTICE 2

Start or Continue Your Judgment Journal – Try and notice any judgments or other disconnecting habitual thoughts you have throughout your day and write them down.

Later on, when you have time, read over your journal for the day. Next, check in with yourself about how you feel as you think about those thoughts. Then look at the Needs List and wonder what need(s) you are trying to meet (or are meeting) with those thoughts.

Then write down at least one other way that you could possibly meet your need(s) that might leave you more connected or at peace.

CHAPTER 10

THE CONCEPT

WHAT EMPATHY IS...
AND WHAT IT'S NOT

"The hearing that is only in the ears is one thing. The hearing of understanding is another. But the hearing of the spirit is not limited to any one faculty, to the ear or the mind. Hence it demands emptiness of all of the faculties. And when the faculties are empty, the whole being listens. There is then a direct grasp of what is right there before you that can never be heard with the ear or understood with the mind."

— Chuang-Tzu

E mpathy is the basic practice that brings me to compassion. It is ultimately quite simple, and quite challenging.

As a child growing up, and for most of my adulthood, I learned to listen with my mind, often with a purpose other than connecting to the person I was with. As I listened to people, I would focus on the future, "What can I say back?" or "What can I think of to fix this?" Other times, I would go to the past, "What does that remind me of?"

50

When I thought these things I became distracted from the moment, more disconnected and *less* able to understand what the other person was experiencing. Then I discovered empathy.

Empathy is the exploration of our human experience – our feelings, our needs – our life-energy trying to emerge and guide us. It is the mindful questioning, the wondering and the genuine curiosity about what we or someone else is going through.

This may sound strange, but I have witnessed over and over again, that this search, or wondering, is the stuff of connection on a deeper plane, and sometimes, even an opening of spiritual space.

The ability to be present in this way challenges many of us twenty-first century humans, highly trained in thinking – as opposed to simply listening. Often, when we are trying to be empathic (even in situations where we are feeling compassionate), we may say things that do not connect us with the other person as well as empathy might.

We may choose to have *non-empathic* forms of communication as part of our lives – and of course, many can serve us wonderfully – they're just *not* empathy. They tend to fill the space, they do not tend to open it up. Becoming aware of these *non-empathic* forms of communication can help us make choices to have a deeper connection when we want it.

To illustrate, below is a quote – something we may hear from a friend, followed by some examples of *habitual, non-empathic* responses that can prevent us from moving to a deeper connection. This is not to say these forms of communication are "wrong" – they're just not empathy. Do any of these responses to the following quote sound familiar?

"Sometimes I just hate my job. My boss is such a control freak."

COMPARING AND ONE-UPPING

"Yeah, mine too. *My* boss is the *worst*. She makes going to work a living hell. I remember a time when…"

Often, when people share what's going on for them, it reminds us about our situation. We may, without thinking about it, share that experience. So think about it – did we just change the subject? Are they telling us this to elicit our experience? Probably not.

EDUCATING AND ADVISING

"Oh yeah, I know what you mean. You know there's this great book called, 'How to Love a Boss that Stinks'"… or "Yeah, when my boss does that, I've learned to…" or "Have you ever tried speaking to the HR department?"

When we hear of someone's pain, we may assume they want us to tell them how to deal with the situation. And of course, we don't like to see people we care about in pain, so we want to help them. Are we doing this to understand what is alive in them or are we working on a fix? Do we expect them to take our advice? And if they don't, are we OK with that? Are we being present to their experience? Probably not.

My friend Marshall Rosenberg told me he only gave advice when it was asked for in writing, notarized, and in triplicate. It helped him stay more present. And of course, advice has a place in life – it's just not empathy.

DISCOUNTING

"That's nothing. In this economy, you should be thankful you even *have* a job."

We may have a *habitual* reaction to try to draw someone's attention to something else in an attempt to "make them feel better". Can you recall a time when you received this kind of response and you thought to yourself, "Oh yeah, that's so true. Thanks for that. I feel better now". I can't.

FIXING AND COUNSELING

"OK. Calm down. Don't worry. We're gonna get through this. I know it feels bad now, but I'm sure it will get better. These things always have a way of working themselves out."

When we hear another's pain, we can feel uncomfortable ourselves and want to somehow fix things. If we check in with ourselves, who's need is that about?

SYMPATHIZING

"Oh, you *poor thing*. I'm so upset when I hear about that. I just *hate* that boss of yours."

Sympathy – the sharing of a feeling through an imagined shared experience – is *different* than empathy. It's kind of like responding to a drowning person by jumping into the water and drowning with them. Yes, it may let them know that you get what is going on for them – it's just not empathy.

DATA GATHERING AND INTERROGATING

"So tell me, exactly what did he do? Has he done this before? Have you noticed a pattern here?"

Data gathering is often a precursor to advising, the warm up to fixing it all. It may come from a sense of *our* curiosity or *our* discomfort with their pain. We may have a genuine interest, to be sure – it's just not empathy.

EXPLAINING AND DEFENDING

"Well, as a boss myself, I know sometimes we just need to crack the whip. He's probably under a lot of stress and doesn't really mean anything by it. It's really hard to be a boss with all that responsibility."

Sometimes *we* are triggered by someone else's pain. This can be especially true in situations when we think we are "to blame" or *responsible*. In these moments, we can become more concerned with our side of the story – *our* need to be understood. This often results in what I call TTNRS: "two transmitters, no receivers syndrome". Sometimes we call it "a fight" – it's certainly not empathy.

ANALYZING

"So where else in your life does this show up? Have you ever considered that this is a pattern for you? Perhaps it's because of your unfulfilled relationship with your father."

Sometimes we are so interested in "getting to the bottom of things" that we forget about the top. Our urge to understand in order to fix *our* discomfort with someone's pain can have us rushing to our brains for answers. Or maybe we have dealt with our own pain this way. No doubt, there are places in life where analyzing is important – it's just not empathy.

SO WHAT THEN? PERHAPS EMPATHY

I'm sure none of us has ever said anything like these examples (*wry smile*). OK, I know *I* have, and likely will again. The difference now, is that when I have the awareness of what I'm doing, I have the choice to do something else – if I want to.

I can recall times, before I developed my empathic skills and my trust in the power of empathy, when the experience of wanting to connect and not knowing how, left me frustrated, confused, and disconnected against my will.

This is where empathy comes in. In the beginning it can be *so* hard to refrain from these *habitual* ways of thinking and speaking. Our *robot* kicks in and away we go, like always.

Now we have a chance to add a new way of being to our lives – a new skill to create a new level of connection – empathy. Shifting to this new focus on feelings and needs is rarely easy. I know for me, it is a life work – one that has given me some of the most beautiful moments of my life.

IN PRACTICE

THE CAR, THE CLUBS, AND THE CAB DRIVER

A few years back, when I was living in Manhattan, I loaned my car, a station wagon, to a friend who needed it to move into her new apartment. We had agreed that she would return it early that evening. That evening I waited to hear from her. I waited […] and waited […] and waited some more […] No call, no car. I drifted to sleep waiting on my couch.

At about *two-thirty* in the morning, I was awakened by a phone call. "Thom, I just finished moving and I just don't have the energy to return the car tonight."

Still a bit groggy, I inquired, "Where did you leave it?"

She informed me that it was parked on a street in the Meat Packing District – with my golf clubs in plain sight in the back. Ten minutes later, after some serious self-empathy (that's a story for another time), I was headed to rescue my car and my precious toys.

I staggered out into the warm rainy night. After a seemingly endless effort, I found a cab. I climbed in, told him my destination, and we headed out – along the edge of Manhattan Island, down the West Side Highway. As we drove along side the Hudson River, we passed the USS Intrepid, a decommissioned battleship that functions as a floating museum.

The driver spoke. "The last time I saw that ship, I was stationed in Viet Nam." From my place in the back seat I could only see the cab driver's eyes, reflected in the rearview mirror.

We made eye contact in the pale gray light.

I replied, "That must bring up quite a bit for you."

After a pause he spoke. "It does."

I listened into the silence that followed. More eye contact, more space. After a time, he spoke again. "When we came back, everybody hated us."

I sat, leaving a quiet space, as the tires thumped rhythmically on the seams of the road, sounding eerily like a beating heart – space for his pain, his need for being seen, for appreciation, for love. I watched the pain slowly seep into his occasional glance.

I spoke. "I imagine that was tough, risking your life like that. I bet it would have made a big difference to have gotten even *some* appreciation."

"Yes... Yes, it would have."

Still seeing only his eyes in the mirror, I watched as the tears slowly filled his eyes. We continued our ride, without speaking a word, as we rolled through the empty streets to our destination.

A few minutes later we arrived. I reached through the little glass hatch and paid the fare – and with compassion and connection in my heart, said a simple "Thank you". I swung the door open and started on my way. From behind me, I heard the sound of the cab door opening. As I turned, there was my newfound friend, walking towards me with an outstretched hand, a look of pure relief in his eyes, and the simple words, "Thank *you*." We shook hands and parted.

I will never forget that ride. Never.

PRACTICES

PRACTICE 1

Increase Your Awareness – See if you can notice yourself using any of the mentioned *non-empathic, habitual* forms of communication. Later, when you have some time and space, see if you can imagine what an *empathic* response would be. What was that person feeling? What was that person needing, wanting to have more of, or yearning to experience? Check the Feelings List and the Needs List for the answer. Now imagine what you might say.

PRACTICE 2

Play the Empathy/Non-Empathy Game – To do this practice you will need a piece of paper and something to write with.

First, write down a quote, something you might say when you would want some empathy, like "I'm feeling really stressed about my finances." *Hint: Don't pick something too important – you'll understand why very soon.*

Read your quote and write down any *non-empathic* forms of communication you may receive (mentioned in this chapter). This could be something like, *comparing*: "Oh you think your finances are bad? I've been broke for…" – or *educating*: "The way I see it, there's a lesson in this for you" – or *discounting*: "Just relax, you'll be fine" – or *data gathering*: "Tell me exactly when this all started."

Next, read the same quote again and write down an empathic response. This could be something like, "Are you feeling scared because you need more peace of mind?"

For this practice, it may be easier to start out with the simplest form of empathy, "Are you feeling _____ (feeling from the Feelings List) because you need more _____" (need from the Needs List).

CHAPTER 11

THE CONCEPT

CREATING YOUR LIFE
OF COMPASSION

"Nothing happens until something moves."

— Albert Einstein

Knowing the concepts and practices we have learned about throughout the book didn't really make much of a difference in my life... until I did them. It is in this area that most of us have our greatest challenge.

THIS CAN BE HARD

As we have discussed previously, many of us are deeply challenged to create new habits and replace our old ones. Our *robot* selves can still be running the show while we struggle to direct our consciousness to a more compassionate place. This can be so challenging that it's easy to give up trying. It's easy to *not notice* that we have slipped off of our barely tread-upon path of awareness, back onto the super highway of judgment, blame, and other forms of habitual thought.

In previous chapters, we have laid the groundwork to create a more compassionate existence... Really. And from that we have an opportunity to build, grow, integrate and refine. We can think of this as our moment of truth.

JUDGING CAN BE EASY

I grew up in a world where judgment was quite normal. I am extremely well practiced at it. I am practiced at thinking that I, and others around me, *should* or *shouldn't* do certain things, all without checking in with the wisdom of my heart. As I shared with you in Chapter 3, I grew up in a world where my feelings and needs didn't matter – for years, many years. So if I'm going to create a compassionate life, I am called on to undo, relearn, fail, succeed, fail again, and succeed again – striving to give myself and those around me this (at times) elusive gift of compassion.

So what does a compassionate life look like for real?

STARTING OR JOINING A PRACTICE GROUP

Practice groups range from small in-person gatherings, to phone calls, to online interactions. Through repeated, communal practice, we can more readily integrate our learning into real life. By sharing exercises, struggles, and successes with one another, we can provide the content and support that helps us develop and use the skills to practice compassion in our daily lives.

GETTING AN EMPATHY BUDDY

The main purpose of an empathy "buddyship" is to simply give and receive empathy – to make it a regular practice in life. In my experience the best way to create a successful buddyship is to find someone who you feel has a similar skill level and a similar learning/ growing rate as you do. Then start with a single call. Give one another feedback about what worked and what you would like to have experienced differently. *Then*, see if you would like to have a second call – then a third, and so forth until you can both comfortably agree to buddy up. Then, choose a mutually agreeable time to speak every week.

The amount of time you spend on these calls may vary. However, you may want to plan on at least forty-five minutes to an hour. The idea is to *exchange* empathy with both taking a turn providing empathy for the other. In my experience, a one-sided empathy buddyship will not last. It's important to have mutuality for sustainability. After thirteen years, I still check in with my buddies about our sense of mutuality.

HAVING EMPATHY MEDICS

Your buddy is there for you during your empathy calls, but may be unavailable at other times. Having at least two "empathy medics" can provide the extra support and relief you may need to live more compassionately. Empathy medics are occasional empathy partners who I can reach out to when my empathy buddy is not available.

TRAININGS AND WORKSHOPS

Trainings and workshops are a wonderful way to renew and deepen our practice. Living, learning, and practicing in community is a powerful and often transformative experience. The synergistic affect of others, the sustained experience, practice, and support of our kindred spirits, create a unique and wonderful experience that can be highly supportive of our growth and practice.

IN PRACTICE

IT FEELS PERFECTLY NORMAL NOT TO GET EMPATHY

I can recall a time about twelve years ago, when my empathy buddy and I fell out of contact. We had been speaking every week for over two years when I went out of town on vacation.

When I came back, we just kind of let things go. After a couple of weeks, I noticed I was feeling cranky and disoriented. I couldn't figure out what was going on. My life seemed normal enough. I wondered, what was up with me?

Then it dawned on me. I was no longer getting my weekly empathy. It was *so* easy to not notice. Like I said, my life seemed normal.

That's when I realized I wanted to have an abnormal life – a life that includes empathy – always, as part of my experience here on earth. I called her and we reconnected. I could feel the difference right away and we've kept up ever since. To this day I remember how easy it was to fall out of that relationship – and how important and precious our time together is.

PRACTICES

PRACTICE 1

Reminding and Remembering – Consider rereading earlier chapters and repeating some of the practices that you imagine will help you grow.

Practice 2

Find an Empathy Buddy – See Appendix F for the link to our Empathy Buddy Forum. This is a perfect place to post a request to find a buddy.

Practice 3

Join or Start a Practice Group – For a free comprehensive 9-week introductory guide and curriculum go to Appendix F.

Practice 4

Attend an In-person Workshop – In-person workshops are also a wonderful place to make a connection. See Appendix F to learn about our Educational Network.

CHAPTER 12

THE CONCEPT

SLOWING DOWN

I magine you have begun to study a new language, like Mandarin. Then imagine being asked to participate in a *real-time* debate in that language, after just a few weeks of study. Yikes, wouldn't that be difficult? OK, maybe impossible.

Then imagine you could stop and take some time between each exchange, translate what you've heard, do some research, figure out what you want to convey, practice what you are going to say, and then speak – more doable, right?

I find that this is a perfect analogy for the work we are learning in this book. The language of compassion is a new way to think and speak. So does it make sense to slow it down? I know it does for me.

There's an expression, "Take time to smell the roses." In our work of moving toward a more compassionate life, we could change that to "Take time to feel the feelings."

Our brains are fast. They're really quite amazing – the ultimate biological super computer. I call my brain my "Maserati". FYI, that's a *really* fast car. If I had one, it would be difficult for me to leave it in the garage. I would most likely take it out and drive.

I think sometimes we're the same way with our brains. They are very good at what they do and we love to use them. The thing is, they can make it hard to slow down enough to do something else – like feel our feelings – or connect our feelings to needs – or wonder what others are feeling and needing.

So in order to give ourselves the gift of compassion, it helps to give ourselves the gift of time and space. This is particularly true in the beginning of our practice, just like when we learn a new language – in our case, the language of compassion.

Imagine you are in a car and you're going a hundred miles an hour, headed straight for a huge brick wall. Would you have any interest in getting out or slowing down and going in a new direction?

I know for me, when I get stimulated or upset (particularly with people who are important to me), it feels like I'm in that car. And when I don't get out or slow down, I always regret it. So I have learned to slow it down. *Slow... It... Down.*

SLOW...

IT...

DOWN...

When I can stop or slow down an interaction that I'm in, I can create the time and space to find my compassion and make room to practice. I can wonder, "What is that?" "What am I feeling?" "What am I wanting to experience right now that I'm not?" With time, I can get to my aliveness, begin to wonder what is alive in the other person as well, and be a more compassionate me.

I have learned that stopping a conversation, or an argument, is one of the greatest gifts I can give myself and those around me. Not like

"The hell with you! I'm out of here!" – more like "I'm feeling so upset right now that I need to take some space to think of what to say."

That said, I know slowing down is not that easy to do. However, it is easier than having a debate in Mandarin… and less painful than driving a hundred miles an hour into a brick wall.

IN PRACTICE

SLOWING DOWN TO STEP UP

Before my studies in compassionate living, I had a habit of getting into yelling matches with my son. When we had a disagreement, we would yell back and forth. This would usually build to a crescendo and we would end up full of anger and pain.

After several months of study with my mentor, Marshall Rosenberg, I was hoping to create a change in this dynamic with my son. Try as I did, I just couldn't seem to come up with the right words to move us to a better connection. If I tried to be empathic, it just came out as mechanical and certainly not sincere. It wasn't sincere because I was usually still angry and awash with should/shouldn't thoughts.

It occurred to me that I needed more time to process.

At that time I had also been reading about anger in a book titled "Emotional Intelligence" by Daniel Goleman. In the book, he explains that certain chemical compounds are released into our bodies when we get angry. The longer we are angry, the more chemicals. Even a moment of anger will release a twenty-minute supply. These chemicals, as it turns out, actually reduce our ability to think, while they increase our ability to act – not a great combination when trying to use a new language in a heated moment.

So I made myself a promise. Whenever I felt angry, I would give myself space and time to recover from my internal dose of intellectual diminishment. I did this by creating at least twenty minutes of quiet time after an "anger attack". The next time my son and I disagreed, it went like this:

"Collin, I really don't want to talk like this anymore. I need time to regroup – so I'm open to trying this again in twenty minutes."

"That's ridiculous," he replied and stormed out of the room. During the time he was gone I gave myself empathy and wondered what Collin must be feeling and needing too. Slowly, carefully, I was able to undertake my exploration.

Twenty minutes later he returned. We started to talk. After about thirty seconds, we were yelling again. I stopped. "Collin, I really don't want to talk like this. I need another twenty minutes."

With a look somewhere between disbelief and frustration, he left again. I gave myself more empathy – more connection and a vision of what I wanted my life to be like in moments like these. I continued to center myself and envision my needs for harmony, understanding, and connection.

Collin returned for our next attempt, and for the third time we began to yell. I called for another twenty-minute break. This time Collin exclaimed, "I'm never coming back!" He left the room, slamming the door behind him.

I sat there, wondering if this was ever going to work – doubting myself and the entire prospect of having a new kind of relationship with my son. I struggled like a drowning man clinging to a rock, struggling to do nothing, except my process of self-empathy and empathy.

To my surprise, twenty minutes later he returned. This time we "held it together" and got through the conversation in a way that was absent of outbursts. It wasn't perfect. It wasn't easy, although it worked. We were able to stop the yelling and fighting.

It was a pivotal moment in our relationship. And yes, we have had our share of upsets after that, although in general, we have held our course and transformed the way we are with each other even today, fifteen years later.

In retrospect it's clear to me, it was the process of *slowing down* that made the difference. Like climbing a set of stairs, it was the step to get to the next place – the place where we could be self-expressed *and* allow the compassion that was always there inside us, to be part of our lives.

PRACTICES

PRACTICE 1

Find Your Moment – Think of a *cue* that you can give yourself when you find yourself getting upset – a way to give yourself space to ask, "What is happening?" Notice how your body feels. Notice the tension or the thoughts that occur in the moments when you are about to "lose it".

You may even want to journal your experiences as a way to recall and deepen your awareness.

Think of a message or phrase you can say to yourself that helps you find your way off of the super highway of upset and onto the path of compassionate, empathic thought and awareness.

You might consider words like "What is that?" or "Wow, this isn't working." or "This is one of those moments." – whatever works for you. The goal is to signal yourself to move to a process of compassionate understanding of yourself and others.

PRACTICE 2

Find Your Words – Imagine what you might say to someone when you notice this moment. How could you slow your conversation down and create the vital time and space to connect to the compassion that awaits inside you? For example:

"I really don't want to talk like this. I need to take some time."

"I'm so upset and I don't want to say anything I'll regret, so I'm taking some time to gather myself."

"I love you so much that I really don't want to talk like this. I need some time to think this out."

"I can't think of a way I can respond that's going to help us right now. I need to take a time-out and talk when I'm more centered."

Note: Three Important Things to Remember:

1) *Don't ask; tell. If we ask for permission, chances are we won't get it. Often, the other person will encourage us to stay in the conversation. It will likely take some compassionate resolve to create the time and space we need. It is especially hard in the beginning.*

2) *Practice ahead of time so you have the words you need within your grasp. Make them your words, remembering they are being said to create compassion and connection. Explain this to others. They may thank you later.*

3) *Let the other person know that you do want to resume. Maybe even provide a time to re-connect. Remember, to the other person "later" can be heard as "never".*

CHAPTER 13

THE CONCEPT

MAKING LIFE MORE WONDERFUL WITH REQUESTS

Throughout the book we've been developing our awareness of "the parallel universe" of feelings and needs. It is this awareness that brings us to a state of "compassionate understanding", for others and for ourselves. From this awareness, or state of compassionate understanding, we are able to move to action in a more connected and constructive way.

Requests are how we connect our compassionate understanding (awareness of needs) to our actions (strategies). Simply put, requests are designed to make life more wonderful for everyone.

WHAT ARE REQUESTS?

In the realm of compassionate thought and action, requests are the way we relate to others and to ourselves, to create change in our lives – in full consideration of our needs, and the needs of others. Big stuff.

For the purposes of this book, we are going to be very specific about the characteristics of a *compassionate request*.

DOABLE

A *compassionate request* is doable. In other words, a request would *not* be to *stop* doing something, it would be to *do* something. Why? Since we know that *everything* we do, we do to meet a need, and needs are the impulses of life – asking someone to simply "stop" doing something is the equivalent of asking them to stop living their life.

In the alternative, if we ask people to meet their needs in a *new* way that might also contribute to *our* needs, we increase the chances of having a life-serving, connected interaction. In this alternative way, others get to keep on meeting their needs *and* we can have more needs met. This is also how we can increase the likelihood that when we attempt to meet our needs with others, it is not at the expense of *their* needs – I know for me, that helps me keep on being who I want to be, all while creating a world I want to live in.

SPECIFIC

A *compassionate request* is specific. "Honey, will you please talk to me like you love me?" Yikes! How do you do that? Even if I wanted to undertake that endeavor, I really might not have a clue what that would look like to them.

I have noticed that people are usually quite willing to contribute to me if it is *not* at their expense. The thing is, it *really* helps when they know *specifically* what that looks like.

For example, "Honey, I'm noticing I'm getting really tense right now. Could we take a two-minute time-out and check the needs sheet on the fridge – and talk about what comes up?"

Now

A *compassionate request* is something that can be done in the present moment. So a *compassionate request* would *not* likely sound like, "Would you keep your room clean from now on?" Realistically, can anyone say "yes" to that and know it's going to happen? Probably not.

A *compassionate request* is more likely to sound like, "Could you tell me what's going on for you when I ask you to clean your room?" That's something that can be done *right now* – not to mention, it's doable and specific.

Needs

A *compassionate request* refers to a need. In my experience, people are more likely to want to contribute to me if they know how it is they are contributing to me (my needs). The more information they have about my needs, the more able they are to make an informed decision. For example, if I say, "Could you tell me what you just heard me say?" this could easily be construed as a *test*. I know it was when I asked my children that. However, if I say, "This is really important to me and I want to be sure I've been clear and we're on the same page. Could you tell me what you heard me say?" – that is likely to create a different, more connecting experience.

Willing to Hear No

Hearing and accepting *no* allows us to live in a different kind of world – where people do things because they want to. We can help create this world of "voluntary living" while continually creating a more and more wonderful life for ourselves and others – *if* we are willing to hear "no".

LIBERATION FROM STRATEGY SCARCITY

Hearing *no* can be really difficult if I have only one or two strategies in my mind. It can seem as though my need will *never* be met if I hear "no". In this situation, fear or hopelessness can set in.

When our awareness is on our *need*, not our *strategy*, we can hear "no" without worrying that our need will not be met. Why? There are *ten thousand* ways to meet any need. That is the liberation we can experience by having "needs awareness". For example, when we're focused on one or two strategies, in our minds we see only these limited choices. When we think in terms of needs, a world of opportunity opens to us. A world where we can hear "no" without it meaning our needs will not be met.

HONORING THE NEEDS OF OTHERS

Additionally, in *compassionate requesting*, we understand that when someone says "no", it means they are saying "yes" to their needs. Remember, anything anyone does, can be seen as an attempt to meet needs – including saying "no".

By hearing "no" from this perspective of needs, we have a greater ability to honor other people's needs, as we pursue the fulfillment of our own.

THE PATH OF REQUESTING

We all know what it's like when someone "has a plan for us" to do something – not a connecting experience. And we all know the pain of really wanting someone to do something they may not want to do – no fun either. Requesting changes all that.

Creating requests absolutely requires an awareness of needs (versus what we want someone to do). If we believe we "need *someone* to…" we would likely be served by receiving more empathy – to get into the awareness of our needs and the *ten thousand* strategies available to us – and get out of the *belief* that any person's actions are a "need" of ours.

Not easy – and yes, doable.

IN PRACTICE

WHAT ARE WE GOING TO DO ABOUT THESE DISHES?

One evening, I came home from work and noticed a pile of dirty dishes in the sink and my son on the couch, playing a video game. Up to this point, what would normally happen in a situation like this was that I would yell and threaten, and most likely, the dishes would get done… and my son Collin and I would be in a state of anger, disconnection, and resentment. So this time, I tried something new.

SELF-EMPATHY

My inner voice: I'd love to trust that when Collin says he'll do the dishes after eating that he'll follow through. I'm also tired and I'd really love to have a sense of order and cleanliness.

I slowed down to take this in for a minute or two […] breathing, *now* also remembering my value for harmony and my desire to have connection with my son.

But yet, there he sat on the couch playing his video game. I started to feel agitated again. I reminded myself that everything we do (even my son on the couch), we do to meet needs. And although I was a bit miffed, I was imagining that a connection to what's going on in

Collin would ultimately be more productive and enjoyable for both of us – certainly more than yelling or threatening.

HONEST EXPRESSION AND EMPATHY

Having taken some time to get centered, I said to Collin, "I would really love to relax right now, and when I see the dishes haven't been washed, I'm noticing I'm getting upset. I would love to have more order and cleanliness, especially after a long day at work. At the same time, I would love to know what's going on for you. I'm thinking it would help if you told me what the deal is with you and the dishes."

CONNECTION

It seemed that Collin could sense my honesty and desire to connect. My *self-empathy* had worked.

Collin: Wow. Thanks for asking, Dad. The truth is I'm exhausted. I get up at *five-thirty* for school, I have tons of homework, I have hockey practice, I have my job eight hours a week, and I'm trying to have a life – I'm just trying to catch a break.

Me inside: I understand. I can relate to being exhausted. He really sounds whipped. I see he really could use a break.

Me outside: So I think I get it, Collin. You're simply at the end of your energy supply and you need a break. Is that it?

Collin: *Yes!* That's it.

I did "get him". I could relate to being tired, wiped out, and exhausted – can't we all?

As our conversation continued, Collin was perking up a bit and we were having friendly eye contact for the first time since I got home.

Me again: Yeah, I get it, kiddo. (We relax a bit. We breathe.) So what are we doing about these dishes?

I remember that moment so clearly. It was so different, the two of us sitting, wondering, "What are we going to do about these dishes?" We were simply sitting and wondering – not fighting.

After a few minutes, Collin turned to me and said, "Wait here. I'll be right back." A moment later he returned with a pen and a piece of graph paper. So with pen in hand and inspiration on his face, he drew a chart of the week with thoughtful detail.

The chart showed that he would be in charge of cleaning the dishes on Monday and Wednesday (non-hockey nights), and his brother would take care of Tuesday and Thursday. Friday was always pizza night, so there was no problem there, and they spent most weekends with their friends or their mother.

From that point on, for the most part, we had resolved the dish problem. And perhaps more importantly, we had gotten through a conflict while staying in connection. I say "for the most part" because there were some *rough spots* over time. That said, by keeping each others' needs in our awareness, we even got through those exceptions with more understanding and less "wrong-making" – a pleasant shift for sure.

You could say, it is the awareness of, and consideration for, the feelings and needs in me *and* others, that makes a request a *compassionate request*. And by using requests this way, I can understand and act on my needs in a way that values and considers the needs of others. Sweet.

PRACTICES

PRACTICE 1

Liberate Yourself – Think of a *no* from someone that you are having a hard time hearing (accepting).

Then, write down what need (or needs) of yours you are trying to meet with the request you're hearing "no" to.

Next, write down 3 to 5 ways you could meet your need(s) *without* hearing a *yes* from that person.

PRACTICE 2

Compassionate Understanding – After you complete Practice 1, imagine what need(s) the person who said "no" was meeting by saying "no".

CHAPTER 14

THE CONCEPT

MORE ABOUT SELF-EMPATHY

How to Be Your Own Best Friend

Of the practices and concepts in this book, *self-empathy* has been the most pivotal and transformational in my life. Without this ability to see my own experience through the lens of feelings and needs, I am missing the valuable information I need to make my life more wonderful. And *that* can block me from caring about others. The journey to compassion doesn't always come with a map. It does however, come with a compass (feelings).

That compass can tell us what our life-energy is calling for (our needs). And with that information we can answer (requests).

The practice of self-empathy creates a basis and ability to see ourselves and others in the light of compassion and, perhaps as importantly, know what we want to do – as opposed to what we think we *should* do.

This dance we call self-empathy offers three ways to connect to ourselves, all of which we have practiced throughout this book. When we use all three, we are empowered to understand ourselves (and ultimately others) in a deeper more life-serving way.

ONE – WELCOME OUR JUDGMENTS

As we discussed in Chapter 8 there is wisdom inside our judgments – it's just not in a particularly usable form. When we can be aware of our judgments, we can *translate* them, by connecting them to our unmet needs. For example:

Judgment Thought	Needs or Values / Things I Love
She's so self-centered	Care, mutuality, consideration
He's lazy	Partnership, support, effectiveness
She's irresponsible	Care, competence, awareness
He's an egomaniac	Self-awareness, presence, mutuality, community, partnership

It is this process of *translating* that makes it useful to welcome our judgments. Remember, if we think we *shouldn't* think judgmental thoughts, we will suppress them and lose the valuable information we need to *unpack* and discover what these judgments are telling us (even though it is in an unusable form at first). Suppressing our judgments would be like taking a rough diamond and throwing it away, thinking, "This is useless."

This is probably a good time to remind ourselves that *welcoming* is different than *sharing*. I cannot remember a single instance when sharing my judgments *about* someone, *with* them, brought us closer together. Imagine saying to someone, "Hey, can we talk about how lazy you are?" It just doesn't work. If I can translate that judgment thought "lazy" into needs – *that* is something I can share while staying in connection. Imagine saying to someone, "Hey, I was thinking I would really love to have more partnership and flow between us. Would you be up for talking about that?" More connecting, right?

I also find it incredibly helpful to remember that my judgments are not "the truth". They are simply an outcry from a part of me that is in pain and cannot express that pain clearly or without blame. For many of us, it is easier and more familiar to judge or be angry than it is to feel our own pain. Compassionate living comes from the understanding that it is more connecting to be sad or curious than it is to be angry. This is a choice.

TWO – FEEL OUR FEELINGS FULLY

As we have discussed before, our feelings have the potential to be our "guides" or "messengers" telling us about our lives. I have noticed that the more I feel my feelings, the more insight I get about what I really want in this life of mine.

My feelings come from within me and are a direct result of how well my needs are doing – how my life is doing. Many of us have learned to suppress or ignore our feelings (see Chapter 3). Some of us judge them or judge ourselves for having them. So it can be difficult to return to this simple practice of *feeling*.

At first, we can work to get to a place where we acknowledge them and feel them. After that, we can learn to stay with them, to go deeply into them – not wallowing in them, but learning from them, being moved by them. This is a practice I will continue to develop for the rest of my life, giving me deeper insight into my needs – into my life.

THREE – FULLY CONNECT TO OUR NEEDS

As you may remember from Chapter 4, needs can be seen as the impulses of life and, in a way, as life itself. Yet much like the wind, we don't ever see these energies – we only experience them and see their effects. We can only feel the wind on our skin. We can only see it moving the leaves in the trees.

So how can we *connect* to these energies in our lives? We can notice and remember our experience of them. We can think about the importance they hold for us and the role they have played and continue to play in our lives. We can see them as separate from the ways they manifest and at the same time celebrate and notice their manifestation. Needs are not the leaves – they are the wind.

One of the practices below is a meditation you can do to develop your relationship with needs. I do this meditation often, with many different needs, and it continues to deepen my understanding of them and my connection to them.

What makes for a wonderful friend? For me, it is someone who provides the space and acceptance for me to vent my judgments, without being judged for it – a person who can see, understand, and allow my feelings, and who understands my needs deeply and without reservation. That can be *me* – *I* can be my own best friend.

IN PRACTICE

ICED TEA

Several years back, I was driving into the city to attend my weekly practice group. I stopped to get myself a quick bite to eat and a nice cold drink.

I pulled off of the road to a "drive-thru" and ordered my favorite burrito and a large iced tea. When I got to the window, I paid for my meal, the server handed me my little bag of food and I drove off, back onto the highway.

As I got up to speed, I realized that I didn't get the iced tea that I had ordered and paid for.

My first reaction was surprise. "How could I just forget?" Then came anger at myself for being so "absent-minded". Next I got angry at the person at the drive-thru window. "How could he just forget? It's his job to do this!"

At that point I was really angry, also disturbed about the two dollars I spent on nothing. Once again, I went back to the judgment thoughts. "My evening is being ruined and it's all my fault. I will *have* to eat this burrito and *suffer* through the inevitable thirst that comes after eating spicy food without anything to drink! Or, I will have to *skip* the burrito altogether, and be *hungry* all night long." I was in a spin.

After a time in this state, I became aware that I was in an old cycle of pain and judgment – one that I had experienced most of my life in situations like this, one that rarely turned out well. With this awareness, I decided to try something else besides going down this path I was on. I checked in with my feelings and needs. What was going on here? I noticed I was frustrated and realized I would have liked to have been more *present* and *competent*. I value these things in myself and I appreciate it when I see them in others.

Thinking about these values of mine, I could feel myself calming down. It occurred to me that perhaps the drive-thru guy may have left the window to get my drink. It also occurred to me that although I wasn't competent or present in that endeavor, I do act in a competent and present fashion most of the time. I began to feel some *compassion* and *acceptance* for myself.

Then I realized that if I had a nice cold iced tea in that moment, I probably wouldn't be going through any of this. This whole thing was mainly because I was hungry and thirsty. In that moment, the two dollars instantly became less important. My slight case of absent-mindedness seemed more acceptable. What I really wanted now was simply something to drink.

Just as this was occurring to me I noticed the next exit on the highway approaching. Two quick turns, two minutes, one "quick-mart" and two dollars later, I had a new iced tea.

My judgments had almost ruled the day. Had I not noticed them, gotten them out, and translated them into feelings and needs, I could have ruined my evening in a battle with myself. Instead I got my iced tea and all was well in my world.

I know this could be considered a "small" example of how self-empathy works. I also know that much of life is made up of "small moments", and it's my consistent and repeated practice of self-empathy that adds up to a more compassionate, connected, and wonderful life.

PRACTICES

PRACTICE 1

Welcome Your Judgments – Think of a situation that is on your mind. In your mind, let out all the judgments, and write them down on a piece of paper. Keep going until you can't think of any more. Then think again. Get them on that paper!

PRACTICE 2

Feel Your Feeling – After completing Practice 1, bring this same situation to your mind. Notice how you feel as you think about it. Pick the feeling that is the most present.

Then feel that feeling. Stay with it. Take your time […] Notice […]

Are you afraid of the feeling?

Are you judging the feeling?

Are you thinking you *shouldn't* feel that way?

Notice anything that may be stopping you from feeling that feeling... and then go back to feeling the feeling. Continue this process for one or two minutes.

PRACTICE 3

Connect to Your Need – After completing Practice 2, identify the need this feeling is related to.

Then, remember a time in your life when this need was met [...]

Create a vision in your mind [...]

What was happening?

Where were you?

What did it feel like?

Stay with this image, like a video in your mind, playing over and over. Bask in it.

Then, after a few minutes, envision a time when someone you know had this need met [...]

Create a vision in your mind [...]

What was happening?

Where were you?

What did it feel like to see this?

Stay with this image, like a video in your mind, playing over and over. Bask in this too.

Stay with the feeling a bit longer. Notice any ideas that occur to you. See if you can think of a request that you might make of yourself or someone else that would move you in the direction of having that need met.

Chapter 15

The Concept

Noticing and Increasing the Quality of Connection

More About Requests

Many of us think about requests in terms of *getting things done* or *action requests*. And indeed, this kind of request is a key to having a more wonderful and compassionate life. That said, there is another form of requesting that enables us to make more life-serving and effective *action requests* – I call them *connection requests*.

What Is Connection Anyway?

We can think of *connection* between two or more people as the existence of four things.

1) I understand and can articulate my feelings and needs.

2) The other person(s) understand(s) and can articulate my feelings and needs.

3) The other person(s) understand(s) and can articulate their own feelings and needs.

4) I understand and can articulate the feelings and needs of the other person(s).

Time after time, I have witnessed that when these four conditions exist, compassion flourishes. There is something beautiful, almost magical, that occurs when this breadth of understanding occurs.

So having the awareness and skill to bring about these four conditions is incredibly empowering when we want to move from a *disconnected state* to a *connected state*. That's where *connection requests* come in.

What Is a Connection Request?

A connection request is a request that is intended to increase the *quality* of our connection with others (and even ourselves). After all, how compassionate can we be when we are discussing things or asking for things from people when we don't know about their needs and they don't know about ours? In order to have a clearer understanding, we can use requests to increase our awareness.

We can look at the *quality of connection* as existing in levels. We can use connection requests to move us through each level, until we have reached a state that we can call *full connection*.

Level Zero

Level zero is when we find out if the person we want to connect with has any interest in speaking with us or hearing what we have to say. This may sound like, "I'm wondering, would you be up for talking about dinner?" After all, speaking to someone that doesn't want to listen is like pushing on a string. It's bound to go nowhere.

LEVEL ONE

Once we are in agreement to speak, level one starts with one person hearing what another person said. We can find out if someone has heard what we said by asking for a reflection. This might sound like, "Would you be willing to tell me what you heard me say"? After all, if the person who is listening didn't hear what we actually said, how much connection can we have? My guess is little to none. The surprising thing about this, for me, is how often we think someone heard what we said when, in fact, they absolutely didn't. If you start checking this out for yourself, I suspect you will be surprised, if not shocked.

I recall the day I found out about this idea some years ago. I immediately started asking my children if they would be willing to tell me what they heard me say. Eighty-percent of the time I got the same response – "Could you say that again, Dad?" I remember coming to the shocking realization that my kids probably didn't hear eighty-percent of what I had said to them for the past sixteen years! It kind of explained a lot (*wry smile*).

LEVEL TWO

After we are comfortable that the other person has actually heard what we said, we can begin to understand what is alive in them, now that they really did hear us.

A level two *connection request* might sound like "Thank you for hearing me. I'm curious, would you be willing to tell me what's going on for you now that you've heard what I just said?" This is where it makes all the difference if we can find out about feelings and needs – not just the words.

LEVEL THREE

Level three is when we make sure we understand what was expressed during level two. That might sound like, "I'd like to be sure I understand you. May I reflect that to you to be sure?" Or "So I think I'm hearing _____." Is that accurate?" If you get a *no* at this point, go back to level two. If you get a *yes* – we are ready to continue.

I also find it helpful if I can reflect what someone has said, especially if I notice I'm feeling stimulated or starting to lose my focus. Reflecting helps bring me back to presence. I want to switch to a conversation with more presence.

To be sure you have completed level three, you may say something like, "Is there anything more you would like me to know?" If you get a *yes* at this point, go back to level two. If there is nothing else, you can continue.

LEVEL FOUR

Level four completes the initial "loop" of a dialog. It is when we share what is going on for us, now that we have heard what the other person is feeling and needing, after they heard us.

This might sound like, "I'm wondering if you have some room to hear what's going on for me, now that I understand what's going on for you?" This cycle of understanding can continue through level five, six, seven, and more, until we reach that place we call "connection" or "compassionate understanding".

Ultimately, when we become proficient in this skill of slowing down, reflecting, asking for reflection, and increasing our connections with others, we will find ourselves in fewer *fights* and way more *dialogs*. It is a way to engage in conflict while keeping our compassion intact.

It's also the way we lay the groundwork for *action requests*. I have experienced over and over again that in this state of *connection* and *compassionate understanding*, action requests seem to fall from the heavens.

And yes, this is very challenging – and it calls on us to be able to self-empathize, empathize, slow down, self-empathize some more, empathize some more, and so on. The thing is – it works.

IN PRACTICE

COULD YOU TELL ME WHAT YOU HEARD ME SAY?

There was a time when my son was out of school, out of work and out of money. He was living with me in my apartment in New York City. At one point I realized he was completely broke, so I decided to give him some money. I also noticed that I was feeling somewhat conflicted because he was smoking cigarettes at the time and I was pretty sure he would use the money to buy some. I also knew that I was no longer interested in coercing him with money (or anything else for that matter). I wanted to support him no matter what he chose to do. That said, I also wanted to share my concern. Our conversation went like this:

Me: Pat, here's some money. I know you need it, so I want you to have it. I also know you've been smoking cigarettes and you're probably going to buy some with this. I just want you to know I'm conflicted.

Pat responded by pushing my cash-filled hand back and saying, "Fine. I won't take it."

Me (surprised): Pat, I'm wondering what you heard me say just now?

Pat: Yeah. I can't have the money if I'm smoking cigarettes.

Me: Whoa! No, I'm *not* saying you can't have the money. It's just that I'm conflicted because I'm pretty sure you're going to buy cigarettes with it. Could you reflect what you're hearing now?

Pat: Sure. I can have the money. I just can't buy cigarettes with it.

Me: Thanks, but that's not it. I said you *can* have it. Do whatever you want with it. I just want you to know I'm conflicted. Could you please tell me what you're hearing "no"?

After a pause he spoke.

Pat: Yeah… You're worried about me.

Me: Yes! Thank you.

I realized that after so many years of coercion, it made perfect sense for Pat to hear my words as just that, even if that wasn't my intention this time. I was so glad we stuck with it and got to where we did – connection.

PRACTICES

PRACTICE 1

Try for Some Connection – The next time you think your message may not have been received, try asking for a reflection. Remember, if you say, "Could you tell me what you just heard me say?" this could easily be construed as a *test*.

If you say something like, "This is really important to me and I want to be sure I've been clear and we're on the same page. Could you tell me what you heard me say?" that is likely to create a different, more connecting experience.

You can also try some of these other requests to build connection:

1) "Having heard what I just said, can you tell me what's going on for you?"

2) "Would you tell me your understanding of my feelings and needs?"

3) "Would you tell me how you're feeling after hearing what I just said?"

4) "Would you tell me what comes up for you about what I just said?"

5) "May I reflect what I think I'm hearing you say?"

6) "May I reflect what I think I heard you say?"

PRACTICE 2

Review and Support Yourself – Review Chapter 13

PRACTICE 3

Requesting Self-Connection – The next time you feel yourself getting upset, ask yourself, "What am I needing right now and not getting?" Yes, as I mentioned earlier, you can make a connection request of yourself too.

CHAPTER 16

THE CONCEPT

SAYING "NO" WITH COMPASSION

Creating Life-Serving Boundaries

I used to think that if I refused to do something, I could be somehow making a demand of someone else. Today I think of it as creating a boundary for myself.

WHAT IS A BOUNDARY?

A boundary is when we say "no" regarding what we are willing or not willing to do (ideally, based on an awareness of our needs). I remember some years back, I was starting to get into a heated discussion with my partner. At one point, it occurred to me that I wanted some space to center myself or the *discussion* was going to become a *fight*.

So I said, "You know, Barb, I need to take a break here." To this she replied, "That's a demand! Because of you, now I can't talk about this." I was puzzled for a moment or two, questioning myself. Was I making a demand? Then it occurred to me, I was setting a boundary.

The difference was that I was not saying what Barb could or couldn't do. I was only dealing with my own actions. This concept started to unravel an idea that I had carried with me most of my life – the idea that I was responsible to do something I really didn't want to do, simply because someone else wanted me to.

So with a new sense of self-connection and understanding I replied, "If you want to talk about it, go right ahead. I'm going for a walk."

My point was clear. I was going to be in charge of me – and for that matter, only me. And if I was going to do anything with or for *anyone*, I would really prefer that it be because I *want to*, not because I *should*.

This turned out to be a benchmark in my integration of compassionate living. I realized that by taking care of myself in this way, I was more empowered to be the person I *wanted* to be as opposed to the person I thought I *should* be. When I did things out of *should*, I almost always felt resentment and pain – and certainly, my heart wasn't in it. It was disconnecting.

Now I have learned to do things because I *want to*. This helps me maintain and act on my self-connection and keeps me more able to be compassionate toward myself and others.

I have expanded this way of living to how I accept support from others as well. It has become clear to me that I don't want anyone else to be doing things that they don't want to either. This act of creating and accepting boundaries continues to change the quality of my life. Much like requests, it empowers me to live in a *voluntary world*, where people (including me) do what we do from our hearts.

WHAT IS A DEMAND?

A demand is when we want someone to do something, without awareness or consideration of their needs. Unlike requests and boundaries, demands don't hold both people's need for choice equally.

As we discussed, I really do want to be able to hear "no", if I want to stay in connection and respect other's needs. Likewise, I want to be able to say "no", so I can have choice and self-expression. From this place of self-expression I can be truly compassionate. Again, if I say "yes" when my heart is saying "no", I will ultimately be resentful and disconnected.

So now I have learned to create and respect boundaries – not just for me, but for the world – to create a world where people act from their hearts.

How Do We Say "No" Compassionately?

Since my first "aha moment" back with Barb, I have learned to say "no" in ways that increase (not guarantee) the odds of a more connected *no*.

These days, in a similar situation, I'm more likely to say something like, "I'm noticing I'm feeling really frustrated and agitated, and I can't imagine I'm going to talk to you in a way either one of us will like. I'm going to take a walk and gather myself so we can really connect later."

Notice in the quote above, I didn't *ask*. I *explained*. If I ask, I could be setting myself up to do exactly what I don't want – when I explain, a clear, yet loving boundary is set.

IN PRACTICE

Saying "No" with Love and Compassion for Both of Us

A number of years ago, I was experiencing a great deal of pain in a friendship that I was part of. This particular friend and I had become friends years earlier, when we had common interests and friends. We were part of a little clan that enjoyed movie-going and other entertaining activities. Now, four years later, it seemed we had little in common. She loved to speak of others and share what she thought was wrong with them. This included our friends, people on the street, public figures – just about everyone.

I realized that this was not a way I wanted to spend my time.

So one day, I asked her if she would be interested in learning to translate these judgments and begin to focus on her own needs and values. After some thought she said, "Not really. I don't think I could do that even if I wanted to… and I don't want to. I like how I am now."

I explained to her that it was painful for me to be around that particular way of seeing things and that I wanted to have a different experience in my friendships.

I also explained that even though I cared very much for her, we would likely be spending less time together. It was not that our relationship was over; it was just going to be different. We cried. We understood. I was saying "no" with love in my heart – love for myself – love for her. It just didn't work for us to be in contact as much.

I mention this because it was a *no*, for sure. It was a breakup of sorts, although it was so different than any other I had ever experienced. It was done with understanding and compassion. She and I still see each other once in a while and it's fine. We don't hold any animosity and we're still happy to see one another at the occasional event.

I could have easily stayed in that relationship, as it was, for years – unhappy, frustrated, and in pain. Or I could have broken it off without the connection – and just let it fade away. I celebrate that I could move away from it with love and compassion for both us. A *compassionate no*.

PRACTICES

PRACTICE 1

Saying "No" Do-over – Think of a time when you said "yes" and you really wanted to say "no". Practice how you might say a *compassionate no* next time.

PRACTICE 2

Try Saying "No" – The next time you think you might not want to do something, check in with yourself and see what needs you would meet by saying "no". Then consider sharing these needs and your *compassionate no* with the other person.

For example, you could say, "I'm thinking we're about to get in a fight right now, and I'm going to take a time-out so we can continue without the fighting."

Or

"I'm conflicted. I would really love to go out and have some fun tonight, but I know I really need some rest, so I'm going to pass. Another time, if you'd like, for sure."

PRACTICE 3

Review and Support Yourself – Review Chapter 12.

CHAPTER 17

THE CONCEPT

COMPASSIONATE USE OF FORCE

Protection versus Punishment

A question that often arises as we begin to study and create a practice of compassion is, "What do we do when things are not happening based on words and rationality?" What do we do when someone is doing something that is harming me, someone else, or themselves? Do we just watch? Do we give them empathy? How do we deal with this? – Really.

If somebody's coming at you with a knife, do you say, "I see you're coming at me with a knife, and I feel scared, and I would love to be experiencing more security, and safety right now, and I'm guessing you're really stressed out and needing some self-expression. Would you be willing to use some other means to express yourself?"

NOT!

Of course, you try to grab their hand and keep the weapon away from you. The question is –what is in your heart as you do this?

PUNITIVE VERSUS COMPASSIONATE USE OF FORCE

The *punitive* use of force is what most of us grew up with. In the punitive use of force, the intention is to change behavior with punishment – with anger, wrong-making, and other forms of judgment in our hearts. In this mode, we are *not* connected to our needs or values. This punitive way of using force is prevalent today in many cultures. It affects the way we treat our children, how we deal with crime, and how we engage in war.

For example, let's think about how we might interact with a three-year-old boy that has just run into the street.

In the punitive use of force, we might grab the child and say, "Bad boy! I'm really angry with you! You're not supposed go in the street! I'm going to teach you a lesson and put you in your playpen and you're going to be there for the afternoon!" In this mode, our three-year-old has learned he is "bad". He has experienced the anger and judgment of an adult (often his life-support) *and* has learned that he *shouldn't* go in the street when grownups are around.

In the protective use of force, we would *also* grab the child. Only this time we might say, "Oh my goodness! That was so scary for me! I was afraid that you were going to get hurt by the cars that drive there! I'm going to put you in your playpen this afternoon so I can relax and you can be safe."

In this instance, the child didn't do anything "wrong". We're not trying to punish him in retaliation for his actions. In this case, we're responding to our value for his safety. In this scenario he has learned that we care about him and that it is dangerous in the street. In this case, the *protective* use of force sheds light on the needs that are causing our behavior, whereas the *punitive* use of force really doesn't.

This is an important distinction on a social level too, when looking at how we operate most of our criminal justice systems. For example, if someone takes something that belongs to someone else, we usually punish them by putting them in jail. This makes it more difficult for convicted people to get a job (and financial security) when they get out. This in turn makes it more likely that they will feel compelled to repeat the act, and the cycle continues. These punitive strategies don't address the problem (the unmet needs). Often, they make it worse.

In the protective use of force, we would address the needs that the person was attempting to meet, even though we may not like how they were doing so. This is the case in "restorative justice courts" (of which there are about twelve in the United States). In these courts, people are often offered job training as an alternative to jail. For example, a "sentence" might be to learn computer repair skills, or a word processing program. This allows people who have broken the law a better chance to meet their needs in ways that are less costly to themselves and those around them.

This distinction of *protective* versus *punitive* use of force creates a new way to bring compassion and care into our lives and our communities when people have done things that we really don't like. When we can move from judgment and hatred to the awareness that we are all just trying to meet our needs, we can live in a more compassionate world and protect life at the same time.

IN PRACTICE

PROTECTING MY POSSESSIONS IN THE PARK

A number of years ago, after I had begun studying and practicing compassionate living, I was walking home after a training, through Central Park in New York City. As I was strolling through a wooded area by the rowing pond, a young man ran past me and grabbed my shoulder bag (which held my laptop computer, my day-planner, my wallet, and a lot of other very valuable things).

I responded in a lightning fast manner and managed to grab hold of the shoulder strap before he could run off with my stuff. Suddenly, I was in an intense "tug-o-war" with this guy, struggling to keep my bag.

Fear and force raced through my body as I yanked and heaved with every ounce of strength I had. I was determined to keep my bag. The struggle continued as we positioned, pulled, and grunted with effort, barely making eye contact. Suddenly, he gave up. He let go of my bag and ran off.

I stood there shaking. I was in shock. It was over as quickly as it started. My body was awash with adrenaline. I could barely believe what had just happened. Then, I noticed something.

I was *not* angry. I was *very* upset – and at the same time, I was *not* hating this person who just tried to take my valued possessions. Yes, I was a mess – and yet, I felt no ill will toward this person. It occurred to me that although I was determined to stop him from taking my bag, I didn't have to hate him for trying to take it. I just wanted to stop him. Somewhere inside me, I knew he thought this was what he needed to do. I didn't know the specific reasons why and yet I knew, in that moment, this was the only way he could think of to meet his needs.

I surprised him and myself that day. And I was able to protect myself in a very forceful way, without hatred or disconnection; simply with the desire to look after my own well-being. I had engaged in the protective, yet compassionate, use of force. I slept well that night.

PRACTICES

PRACTICE 1

Use of Force Do-over – Think of a time when you used punishment in a forceful way. Imagine how you might have been able to approach the situation using a *protective* use of force.

PRACTICE 2

Try Something New – The next time you think you need to *punish* someone, think of what you are trying to accomplish. What are you trying to *protect*? See if you can think of a way to do that without anger in your heart.

CHAPTER 18

THE CONCEPT

BELIEFS AND NEEDS

Working with Habitual Thoughts

I n my study and practice of compassion, I have developed the ability to see all actions as an attempt to meet needs. I've also learned to see beliefs as an attempt to meet needs too. They help me interact with my perceptions and explain and understand my life.

A TALE OF TWO BELIEFS

Belief one – "I'm lazy." When I was younger I believed I was lazy. I thought it was simply "the truth" – and *not* a belief. Later, as I developed a more empathic view of myself, I realized I was using this belief to motivate myself (a need for inspiration). I could also recall troubling moments where I used this thought, "I'm lazy," to explain my behavior to myself (an attempt to meet my need for understanding).

Belief two – "I don't deserve to have my needs met." With a shift toward empathy this thought can be seen as an attempt to protect myself from disappointment (a form of self-care). It can also be seen as an attempt to understand why my needs are not met (again, an attempt to meet a need for understanding).

EMPATHY FOR BELIEFS

This practice of looking at beliefs as an attempt to meet needs provides a way to understand myself and others that includes more compassion and deeper understanding. And that offers me previously unknown ways to make my life more wonderful.

This is not to say that having thoughts or beliefs is a "bad idea" or that there is something inherently "wrong" with them. As humans we are bound to have them. This is to say that when I think about a belief in relation to my needs, it gives me a way to decide if my belief is serving me or not. This is big.

Let's look at a common belief. Some people believe that "People are basically selfish, that they are ultimately out for their own good and we have to be on guard – that we have to protect ourselves from them." We could argue that this is true – or not true – probably forever.

If I look at this belief through the lens of needs, I might discover that this is a way I take care of myself – a way I protect myself from people and to be more assured that I will be safe.

I can also wonder, "What need(s) of mine am I not contributing to by having this belief?" I can wonder if it is contributing to an experience of trust, closeness, or compassion. I can ask myself, "Is this belief keeping me from experiencing intimacy?"

When we can think about our beliefs in this way, we can create a new relationship between our minds and our hearts. We can examine any belief from a *needs perspective* and see something we have never seen before.

This process of examining my beliefs in relation to needs has had a profound, life enriching effect on my relationships – with myself, the people in my life, and the world in general. Through this process, I have been able to choose my beliefs and not be run by them.

IN PRACTICE

MY MIRACLE WEDNESDAY IN CENTRAL PARK

One of the finest, growth provoking experiences I have ever had, was the result of looking at my own beliefs about myself – who I am and what kind of person I see myself as.

It was a Wednesday night in New York City. That night, there was a free concert being given by "Sting" in Central Park. There was talk that other well-known artists would be there as well. However, there was a hitch. Even though it was free, I still needed to have a ticket, all of which were taken through the various outlets (radio stations, record stores, etc.). And I didn't have one. That said, there was a rumor that some tickets might be given out at the gate, so maybe I could get in.

There was another problem. I didn't have anyone to go with. This presented a great conflict for me. At that time, I had a belief that, "I don't go to concerts alone."

As the time passed and I couldn't find a partner to go with, I was confronted by the fact that this belief could keep me from seeing a potentially great concert. In that moment it occurred to me this belief (that I don't go to concerts alone) wasn't working for me – at all! So I decided to let go of it and believe that I was a person who did go to concerts alone.

I headed for the gate. When I got there, I found out there were no tickets being given out. The man at the gate said, "If you want a ticket, you're going to have to ask someone if they have an extra to sell you or give you." This presented my next challenge. I also held a belief that, "I'm not the 'kind of person' that walks up to strangers and says 'got an extra ticket?'" For that matter, I believed I wasn't the "kind of person" that walks up to strangers and says anything!

For a second time that evening, I was challenged to see my beliefs as something besides "the truth", and examine them in terms of what needs they met or did not meet. Bottom line, if I wanted to attend this concert, I was going to have to let go of this belief too. I did.

I started to believe I was someone who walked up to strangers and asked for things. I started. "Got an extra ticket?" "No." "Got an extra ticket?" "No." "Got an extra ticket?" "No." This was tough – although getting a bit easier as time went on. After ten minutes I got a "Sure." "Twenty bucks OK?" "OK."

I was going to the concert!

Because I went alone, I was able to get a seat right in front of the stage. It was an amazing performance. The music was so beautiful and lively that I decided to let go of one more belief. I let go of the belief that, "I don't dance." I danced – yes alone – and had the time of my newfound life.

PRACTICES

PRACTICE 1

Inventory Your Beliefs – Write down a list of beliefs that you have. For example, "The world is a dangerous place," "The world is a safe place," "People are basically compassionate," "People are basically self-centered," "I am not good enough," "I don't deserve a rewarding relationship," and so on. *Really* check yourself out. Write them down.

Under each belief, write a list of needs that are met and needs not met by that particular belief.

PRACTICE 2

Think of a New Belief – After Practice 1, see if you are really getting what you want from your beliefs. Then, if you can find one or more beliefs that are not serving you as well as you would like, try writing down some new beliefs. Make a list of needs that are met and needs not met by these new beliefs too.

> *Note: This is a practice that we can all engage in for life. It takes repeated practice and it often helps to get support from an empathy buddy. The results are almost always wonderfully life-changing.*

CHAPTER 19

THE CONCEPT

THE ART OF OBSERVATION

"I think that my job is to observe people and the world, and not to judge them. I always hope to position myself away from so-called conclusions. I would like to leave everything wide open to all the possibilities in the world."

— *Haruki Murakami*

As I wrote in Chapter 2, as a little human growing up, I learned to behave through *judgment*, as did many of us. I was taught to do things because they were "the right thing" to do, or not to do other things because they were "the wrong thing" to do. I learned that if I behaved in certain ways, I would be deemed a "good person", and if I behaved in other ways, I would be deemed a "bad person". I also learned that I *should* do some things and that I *shouldn't* do other things.

As I grew up in this environment, judgment helped me to fit into society. It helped me belong, stay safe, and understand. Yet, at the same time it did not help me develop a sense of self-connection or compassion very well.

I learned that I (and others) could be considered "stupid", "selfish", "lazy", or any number of judgments. These terms helped motivate me – by fear – to behave differently. And although this accomplished that – again, it did not work very well in helping me experience connection or compassion.

WHAT DO JUDGMENTS HAVE TO DO WITH OBSERVATIONS OR COMPASSION?

As we have discussed numerous times before, with practice, we can learn to translate our judgments, to find out about our needs. There are needs connected to every judgment, and when we identify them, it gives us a chance to have more connection in our conversations. I say *a chance* because having the awareness of our needs is the *first* step to a connected conversation. The *second* part is to be able to express ourselves in ways that reflect our awareness. So how can we talk about the actual situations, events, and people in our lives without using those very same judgment words we grew up with? Observation.

Observation is an *alternative* that we can use when we want our consciousness and conversations to move from judgment to connection and compassion. If I can't think of an observation – a neutral, judgment-free way of thinking and speaking about something that I or someone else did – I probably need more empathy, to get to a clearer understanding of my needs and the actual event or events that are at issue.

For example, imagine I said to my friend, "Hey listen. You know when you were yelling and complaining to me about your car keys yesterday?" My friend might say, "I was not yelling! I was just being emphatic!" As you may see, this conversation could easily turn into a debate about *how* he was speaking – not *what* was said, or how it was for anyone.

Now imagine I said, "Hey listen. Remember when we were talking about how I lost the keys to your car yesterday?" It is much more likely that my friend will be able to focus on the actual event and move on to a more connected conversation.

How Can I Be Sure I'm Making an Observation?

A little thought I use to figure out if I'm *observing* or *judging* is by checking, "Could I capture that on a video camera or in a written transcription?" In our example above, "yelling" and "complaining" are subjective or evaluative terms. Yes, we could capture that an elevated volume level was used, although it gets a bit unwieldy to say, "When you were speaking at twenty-five decibels...".

Tone of Voice

In the discussion of *observation*, it becomes a bit confusing when we want to acknowledge that we are hearing a different tone of voice. How do you *observe* that someone *seems* agitated or angry or frustrated? Often these are things we pick up on by *tone*, right?

The best way I have learned to stay in *observation mode* and still express what I think I'm hearing is:

1) Ask. For example: "So is it that you're really frustrated that I lost the keys to your car?"

2) Observe your reaction. Sometimes I have the thought that someone is being "condescending" or "sarcastic". These are certainly not observation words, and yet I want to address what is going on in me – to create a space for self-empathy, to translate my interpretation into needs and a request. In this case, I can observe that I am having a reaction to their tone. "I'm noticing I'm having a reaction to your tone of voice and

I'm having a hard time hearing what you're saying right now. Could we take a minute to check in or take a breather here?" (see Chapter 12)

I know this is not always going to work perfectly, since I can never control how someone is going to react to me. I can only know I'm doing the best I can to get to a connected place and go on from there. Sometimes I can simply hear their pain and in so doing, the *tone* of what they're saying becomes less important to me and allows me to stay connected or get reconnected to them.

IN PRACTICE

PAT'S ROOM

Some years back, when my younger son was in his early teens, I often found myself in conflict with him over the condition of his room. I was mostly concerned by how "messy" it was. He was mostly annoyed by my concern.

This state of affairs existed for months, maybe years. At one point, after I had been studying with Marshall Rosenberg for some time, I began to translate my judgments into needs and speak in terms of observations.

As I walked by Pat's room one morning, I decided to think about my *observation* instead of my *judgment*. My judgment had been that it was messy. I also had a judgment that he *should* keep his room "neat". I decided to find an *observation* and a *need*. This process created a deeper understanding of what was going on in me and ultimately, I experienced a shift in perspective and experience. I was "chilled out" with my new perspective and was able to let go of my judgments and connect through observation and needs.

Our next conversation about his room was completely different than any we had engaged in before.

Me: So Pat, I've been noticing that you put your clothes on the floor after you wear them. I've also been trying to figure out why I've been having such a reaction to that. It occurred to me that it's because I really have a thing for order and ease and I'd like to tell you about it.

Patrick: Dad. I know it bugs you. I can just keep my door closed. But what do you mean ease? You don't have to pick it up.

Me: No, it's not that. I remember that when I used to throw my clothes on the floor, I would lose track of what I had to wear. And also that I ended up moving them twice, once to the floor and then again to the hamper, twice the work.

Patrick: Hmmmmmmm.

Me: Anyway, for now I'm OK with the door closed.

This was perhaps the most rewarding, connecting conversation Patrick and I had ever had about his room. I was able to clearly share my needs with him, a great relief. And, as long as it didn't reach "health hazard" proportions, I was OK to simply leave his door shut.

Three days later, I noticed Pat's door was open. As I looked in, I could see the floor of his room for the first time in a long time. There was something different this time. Pat had moved his clothes because he wanted to, not to avoid my judgment. A floor free of clothing and conflict. Sweet.

PRACTICES

PRACTICE 1

Review the "Shifting Toward Compassion" Exercise – This time, work with this exercise using *observations* in addition to, or instead of, quotes (see Appendix C).

PRACTICE 2

Distinguishing Evaluations and Judgments – (Review of the "Translating Judgment into Observation Exercise" from Chapter 6) – This exercise helps us find the "hidden judgment" inside the way we use words. It is also practice in speaking in a judgment-free manner (see Appendix E).

CHAPTER 20

THE CONCEPT

SCARY HONESTY

Creating a New Level of Connection

Scary honesty is when we tell someone what is really going on for us, even though we are afraid of how they might react. You could say it's a way of being *courageous* in our desire and actions, to create a deeper connection with someone.

This form of honesty may show up as an interruption, or a question, or a statement about something that is going on inside us. It is *always* intended to create a deeper, more compassionate, more connected relationship.

Have you ever been in a conversation where the other person was going on and on about something that you really didn't care about, and yet you kept listening anyway? Have you ever been in a conversation when someone has said something that offends your values, and yet you kept quiet, letting it pass nonetheless? Have you ever said *yes* to someone because you were too uncomfortable to say *no*, even though you really wanted to say *no*? Have you ever eaten something you didn't like, for fear of offending your host? Most of us have. And do you recall these experiences being connecting or disconnecting? I know for me they are often painfully disconnecting, particularly when it is with someone I care about or want to be close to.

Scary honesty is something I can use when I'm conflicted, wanting ease and harmony, and yet also wanting to have shared understanding or connection.

Scary honesty is a way for me to try for a more authentic interaction at the risk of some conflict.

How Do We Express Scary Honesty?

Scary honesty calls on us to be centered in needs and our intention. Are we wanting to *correct* or *connect*? Are we intending our expression to bring us closer to another person, or is it to *be right*?

Are we self-connected enough to speak about ourselves and our feelings and needs, or are we thinking in terms of judgment about what they are doing or saying?

Scary honesty calls on us to self-empathize to the point where we are clearly centered in our own feelings and needs – *and*, that we are *clear* that we are looking for connection and can speak from that place.

Scary honesty does not sound like, "When I hear you say 'those people', it seems to me that you are being a bigot."

It might sound like, "When I hear you say 'those people', I notice I have a reaction. I think my reaction is because I like to think we are all basically the same, a single human family. That said, I'm conflicted about bringing this up because I don't want to offend you. At the same time I value our connection and would love to be honest with you."

Scary honesty does not sound like, "Sure, I'd love to go out tonight."

It might sound like, "Wow, I'm really conflicted. I've been hoping you would ask me out and we could spend some quality time

116

together. At the same time, I know I have to get up crazy early tomorrow morning and tonight just doesn't make sense for me. Could we go another night?"

When we *don't* share what is really going on for us, we are more likely to experience distance or disconnection from others. When we *do* share our true feelings and needs, it gives us the chance to live a more connected, compassionate life.

IT'S AN OPTION, NOT A "SHOULD"

I like to remember, just because I *can* be more honest and open, it doesn't mean I'm required to be. I like knowing I have the option to self-empathize and create a deeper connection, even if faced with the possibility of conflict – *when I want to*. It doesn't mean I'm going to *work it out* with every bus driver, customer service rep or cashier – *or* when I am exhausted or upset.

However, when I *do* genuinely want more connection and understanding with a friend, or my father, or my partner, being able to express *scary honesty* gives me that option.

IN PRACTICE

INTERRUPTING FOR CONNECTION

My good friend Kenny has a funny habit of talking, almost nonstop, when he gets nervous or excited. It seems to me, he will talk about anything just to keep his jaw moving. As much as I love him, I must admit, this habit has not been a part of our relationship that I like. In fact, in the past, it often drove me nuts. I never found a way to tell him this because I didn't want to "hurt his feelings", and secondly, I usually waited so long to say something that I was too upset, and would have said something I regretted – so I always kept my mouth shut and waited it out.

At one point in my studies, my friend and mentor, Marshall Rosenberg, told me a story that inspired me regarding my situation with Kenny. It was about how he interrupted a friend of his because he wanted to have a stronger connection.

Several weeks later, Kenny and I got together and he started telling me about a wedding he had gone to, and about the music, and about the food, and about the almonds, and about his dry cleaner, and about his cousin's ex-girlfriend, and his aunt's perfume – I was going out of my mind!

I decided to self-empathize. I got clear that I wanted to be experiencing more connection, to have a closer relationship with Kenny in that moment. Part of me was filled with fear. I was taught that it's "rude" to interrupt people. I was afraid Kenny might be offended or hurt if I didn't sit there and listen. This time, I was also filled with the desire and where-with-all to "be real" with my good friend. Out it came.

"Kenny, you're losing me here. I can't seem to pay attention to all these details. Honestly, they just don't interest me." I thought for a moment that Kenny might hit me, or storm out of the room in anger. Instead, he spoke.

"Yeah, now that you mention it, I'm kind of bored too. Let's talk about something else."

I was shocked, relieved, and then jubilant. My *scary honesty* paid off big time. In an instant, our conversion went from a lifeless diatribe, to a truly connected moment.

Since that moment, my relationship with Kenny has had a new feel. It has been a deeper, more connected experience – one I look forward to. And yes, Kenny still "gets going" every now and then, and all I need to do is be honest and the connection returns. Nice.

PRACTICES

Practice 1

Scary Honesty Redo – Think of a time when you were not as honest as you would have liked because you were afraid of the consequences. Think of what you might have said to create more connection.

Practice 2

Scary Honesty in Action – Think of someone who you care about – who often speaks more than you enjoy. Try *compassionately* interrupting them to create more connection in that moment.

CHAPTER 21

THE CONCEPT

GIVING THANKS

Appreciation from the Heart

As I have worked toward living a more connected and compassionate life, I have developed an ability that I can only describe as a *mega-life-changer*. It is my ability to *appreciate* in a newer and deeper way. It affects almost every moment of every day and changes how I experience the people and events that make up my life.

THE ANATOMY OF APPRECIATION

What is it when something happens and we just want to say "Thanks"? What is happening inside of us? As a student of compassionate thought and action, I have learned that three things are happening in these moments.

First, something just happened (or is happening) – somebody said something, or did something, or there was/is some event in our lives. You could say that there is an *observation* that goes with everything we appreciate. For example, when I woke up this morning, I was warm. I noticed my fuzzy blanket, my soft warm pillow, and the quiet, reassuring morning light peeking through the curtains.

Second, I felt something. In my experience (which has been enriched by my practice of feeling feelings), I always feel some *fulfilled feeling*. In the case of my blanket, my pillow, and the morning light, I was feeling a sense of comfort, hope, and gratitude.

Third, a need is met. In the case of my blanket and my pillow, it was security and comfort. In the case of the morning light, it was hope, support, and communion.

It is the noticing of all these three things that gives me the ability to be in a deeply connected and grateful place.

In this book so far, we have studied and practiced *observation* and *self-empathy*, both of which enable us to recognize these three aspects of our experience. So from this moment on, we can use these skills and practices to change how we experience our lives. More good news – the more skilled and practiced we get at this, the more we will connect with the beauty and fun of being alive. Really.

SHARING APPRECIATION

We can share this skill and awareness with others who may not be practicing it as consciously as we are, yet are still having the same wonderful kind of lives we are. Sharing our appreciation can be profound, like when we share our appreciation with a parent or loved one. It can also be simple, like when we share our appreciation with a customer service person at a store or on the phone. From experience I can tell you, it's always fun.

A little example: The other day I was in my local "Home Center Megamart", the kind that's so big, I would like to have a bicycle to get around in it. A woman who worked there asked me if she could help. I told her I was looking for an electrical outlet for my dryer. She walked me straight to it (the event or observation).

I realized that I could have been looking for that thing for a *really* long time, if it were not for her help (feeling gratitude; needs met for ease, efficiency, and support).

So I said, "Thanks. You just saved me a good ten or fifteen minutes. I could have been wandering all over looking for this." She responded with a look of pleasant surprise and a smile so wide I thought she might hurt her face. It was so rewarding to share that little moment – little and yet quite beautiful.

IN PRACTICE

A HAPPIER FATHER'S DAY

It was Father's Day and I was about to make the usual phone call to my dad. This time I wanted to make it a special call, a more connected conversation than the typical "Happy Father's Day. So how's it going?" I wanted to share an appreciation that was from my heart, not just make the call out of obligation.

Before I called, I took a few moments and thought to myself, "What is it that I appreciate about this man and my relationship with him? What are some of the things that have happened between us? How have my needs been contributed to by his actions and words?" This process brought me to a new and deeper place.

When we spoke, instead of just saying "Happy Father's Day," something else came out of me. "Dad, I realize there have been four stages in my relationship to you. The first was when I just did what you said, the second was when I did what you said and resented it, the third was when I tolerated what you said, and the fourth was when I appreciated what you said. I'm in the fourth stage now, Dad. I'm beginning to notice that the things you said taught me some pretty important stuff – and I'm using that knowledge now – from how to saw a piece of wood, to how to act at a dinner table. Thank you."

After a moment of silence, in a voice trembling in tearful joy, my father spoke. "Well, wow... Thank you for that, Thom."

When I got off the phone, I realized that it was my desire to see the needs that were met in my relationship with my father that gave me a gift – to experience the energy of appreciation inside me. The skills I had developed in *compassionate self-expression* gave me a second gift – the sharing of that appreciation in a meaningful and connected way with someone I love. Add to that, my dad was able to understand how he had made (and continues to make) my life more wonderful – a third gift. It was a wonderful Father's Day.

PRACTICES

PRACTICE 1

Practice Noticing – Write down a list of 5 to 10 things that are happening in this very moment, and the met needs that you are experiencing. For example, breathing (air), reading this (learning and growth), sitting in a building (security).

> *Note: I can NOT express in these few words, how powerful this practice is.*

PRACTICE 2

Share an Appreciation – Remember something that someone said or did that contributed to your needs being met. Ask them if you could share something that you appreciate with them. Then, let them know what happened, how it felt, and what need(s) it met. For example: "I just want to let you know how grateful I am for the help with these dishes. I realize what a difference it makes when we team up like this. It's way more fun, not to mention it goes so much faster when we talk with each other. Thanks."

CHAPTER 22

THE CONCEPT

THE POWER OF THANKS –
MORE ABOUT APPRECIATION

*"The greatest of all gifts is the power to
estimate things at their true worth."*

— *François de la Rochefoucauld*

APPRECIATION VERSUS PRAISE

As a child, I grew up hearing expressions like "good boy" or "nice job". These expressions of *approval* were often nice to hear and yet, always left me wondering. What was "nice" about that? It also left me a bit nervous. Does that mean I might *not* be "good" if I do something else?

These were the instructions I received on how to be a human. It was the *praise* I received from the "people in charge". From this *praise* I learned that certain behaviors earned me the label of "good". They also reminded me that I might lose that label if the "people in charge" decided my behavior *wasn't* "good".

I have come to realize that many of the expressions of *praise* that I have received were often designed to get me to *behave*. Others were designed to let me know that someone appreciated my actions and were grateful for what I did.

The second category felt different. These expressions touched me in a way that felt connecting and clear. These are the ones I want to understand and be part of. They were not *praise*; they were *appreciation*.

LIVING IN APPRECIATION

Using the skills we have learned in this book so far, we can experience a deeper, more satisfying experience of appreciation. Also, as we discussed just a few chapters ago, through language, we can share that experience with others.

Inside myself, I can use the skills of feeling my feelings and connecting them to my met needs, to notice the copious amounts of "metness" I am experiencing throughout my day. Right now, as I write these words, my brain is having thoughts, translating them into words, organizing them into sentences, helping my body type them into the message you are reading, and helping me share this with you. Self-expression – *Mmmmmmm*. All this while I am sitting in my office, which is clearly thirty degrees warmer than it is outside, while I'm fully clothed, while I'm fully rested, while my heart is pumping life through my body, while my lungs are bringing me fresh air, while the trees are helping make that fresh air, while this big blue ball of water, earth and life spins in space, while the sun gives us warmth and light – comfort, security, care, well-being, peace of mind, communion – that's what I'm talkin' about! I can notice this. I can *feel* this. I can see that there are thousands of things happening that are contributing to the "metness" of my needs. I could go on – and I will (although I'll stop for now so I can get back to writing). Simply summarized, the practice of appreciation makes my life, and the lives of those around me, more wonderful.

RECEIVING APPRECIATION

Some years ago, my partner and I had developed a practice of taking a few moments each day to share our appreciation for how we contribute to each other. In the beginning, it was a bit uncomfortable for me. After some self-empathy, I realized it was because when I was growing up, appreciation had usually come in the form of *praise* and *approval* – both of which were used as a form of power over me. It actually engendered a sense of anxiety.

With some practice I learned to receive appreciation like "a shower", as opposed to "sustenance". Appreciation from others has become something that adds to my life, not something I depend on to feel OK about myself. This shift gives me a very different experience, one that is more choiceful and gratifying.

I have also noticed that when we think about the *needs* that we contribute to through our actions – and not *just* the *actions* themselves – our experience becomes deeper and more satisfying.

IN PRACTICE

A MOVING EXPERIENCE

A number of years ago, when I was living on the Upper West Side of Manhattan, I was in my favorite bookstore, a Barnes and Noble on Broadway.

I was lining up to get on the escalator (as is common in the city), and noticed a father and his three-year-old son approaching the moving staircase.

The father was weighed down with a full day's payload of purchased goods, a stroller, and his son, trailing close behind. As "Dad" got on the escalator, juggling his bounty, his son stood there frozen, struggling to find a way to step on, and keep up with his rapidly descending dad. The little boy called out in a frightened, slightly quivering voice, "Dad?"

By the time his father noticed what was happening, he was hopelessly watching the space between them grow – from half way down the moving mass of metal stairs.

Seeing this, I stepped up and held my hand out to the soon-to-be panicking little person at the top of the stairs. I spoke. "Hold my hand." He reached up. "Ready? Here we go." We stepped onto the machine together. And down we went.

As the two of us reached the bottom and stepped onto solid ground, he looked up, straight into my eyes, let out the cutest little sigh of relief, and said perhaps the most heartfelt "Thank you" I have ever heard.

It was so sincere and chock full of deep appreciation, I almost cried from the joy of this wonderful exchange. I feel warm right now re-counting it. I could clearly see and feel what this meant to my little friend. His dad was pretty happy and relieved too. I owe it to my practice of compassion, that this seemingly "insignificant" moment was so wonderful for me. Thanks to my ability to fully connect with this little guy's feelings and the "metness" of his needs in the moment – a moment I will appreciate forever.

PRACTICES

PRACTICE 1

Check In Again – As we did last time, write down a list of things that are happening and the needs that are being met in this very moment. For example: breathing (air), reading this (learning and growth), sitting in a building (security). This time, write down ten to twenty of them. How do you feel?

Practice 2

Appreciate Yourself – Write down 3 ways you contribute to your own life – 3 things that you do or have done that you enjoy. Then write down the needs you meet for yourself. Then look in the mirror and say, "Thank you." *Note: It is difficult to do this without smiling.*

Practice 3

Sharing an Appreciation Renewed – Think of something that someone said or did that contributed to your needs being met. Ask them if you could share something you appreciate with them. Then let them know what happened, how it felt and what need (or needs) it met.

For example: "I just want to let you know how much I appreciate your company at the movies last night… and for that matter all the times we've spent together – the friendship, the fun, and companionship you bring into my life makes such a difference to me. Thank you, really."

You can do this in person, by phone, through an email, or by writing a card.

CHAPTER 23

THE CONCEPT

APOLOGIES VERSUS RESTORATION

*There's a difference between doing something
'wrong' and doing something we regret.*

During my trainings people often ask what role *forgiveness* plays in compassionate living. The answer is always the same. We don't have to forgive someone who hasn't done anything "wrong". Without "wrongness" or blame or judgment in the picture, we are more able to focus on understanding and seeing if there is a way to restore our connection.

WRONG VERSUS REGRET

Throughout this book, we have learned that we can see all actions as an attempt to meet needs, even actions we find objectionable (see Chapter 1). We have also learned that needs can be seen as a driving force behind all judgments, and that when we can focus on those *needs* we are more likely to stay connected, or get back to a connected state, even when people do things we don't like (including ourselves).

We can use this way of thinking to bring our focus to what it is we are wanting to experience, as opposed to what the other person has done "wrong". This, in turn, increases the chances of making compassionate requests and creating a more wonderful and connected life in the future.

We can think this way about our own actions as well (see Chapter 14). When I see myself as "wrong", my focus and awareness is disconnected from my life-energy (my needs), and way more connected to my habitual thoughts and judgments.

Over time, with practice, I have learned to see that when I do things that I judge as wrong, it's because I didn't meet my own needs. By relating to myself on this *needs* level, I can more readily understand that I would like to have done something differently, as opposed to thinking I have done something "wrong". In other words, I can *regret* my actions *without* judging myself.

COMPASSION TURNED INWARD

In judgment, I become disconnected from myself and often experience shame and guilt. When I become aware of my needs, I can more readily focus on *restoring* connection as opposed to "beating myself up".

In *needs consciousness*, I can more clearly see and understand that I was simply being human, trying to meet my needs. I can start to see my own actions in terms of *needs met, needs not met – worked, didn't work.*

From this place of compassion for me I can move toward others. I can express my regrets to them in a heartfelt, connecting way, as opposed to a self-critical and shameful way. I have also noticed again and again, that when I'm in *needs consciousness* I can more readily create a picture in my mind of what I would prefer to do in the future.

IN PRACTICE

KITCHEN DISCONNECT

One day I noticed my partner had put my fine Japanese steel knife in our metal dish rack. When I saw it there I became very upset – OK, I freaked out. In my semi-panicked state I yelled out, "Knives don't go in the dish rack; you're going to ruin them!" From that moment, I watched her go to surprise, then to fear, then anger. She stepped away.

In that moment, it was clear to me things were not going well. I was angry, she was resentful, *we* were disconnected. I could have easily considered my actions to be "wrong". Earlier in my life, this would have brought on shame and guilt – I could have easily retreated to protect myself, or worse, justified my actions by making her "wrong", thinking she "should" have known better. Instead, I noticed the disconnection and looked for a way to bring us back to our normal, more connected state.

With some inner exploration, it occurred to me that my actions reflected little to none of my value for care, harmony, and for that matter, communication itself. I was acting in a way that was not in congruence with what I value.

It also occurred to me that I was in pain. I was thinking she knew about fine cutlery (shared understanding and care), and I was surprised and panicked about protecting my very expensive tool (financial security). Also, this particular knife was a gift from my sons, so it had a special meaning for me (care, love). In the light of this understanding, I could see why I did what I did – I could have some compassion for myself. And without blame occupying my mind, I could also still understand that my response didn't meet my needs for care, harmony, and partnership. So things changed a bit.

I spoke. "You know, when I just said that, it *so* didn't show my care for you or, for that matter how much I value our relationship. I wish I had said something else – certainly in a different way." I waited – no defending, no explaining – simply a focus on my regret.

Silence […] a reply. "Like what?"

"Like, when I see metal knives go in metal dish racks, I worry that they'll get chipped. Could we put them someplace else – like on a towel or in the knife rack?"

More silence […] "OK."

I can easily imagine this interaction could have been much longer and much more painful. This time, because I was able to focus on needs (not blame), and my partner was able to see them too, things got back to their normal, caring, and loving state. Nobody "wrong" – everyone understood. Nice.

PRACTICES

PRACTICE 1

Restoration Preparation – Think of a situation where you said or did something you regretted, and were unable to express yourself in a more connecting way. Perhaps you were feeling too scared or angry with yourself or the other person. Write down how you might say it now, in terms of your own unmet needs. The following steps may help.

1) Observation: Recall an occasion when you did or said something you wish you hadn't; the exact action or quote.

2) Acknowledge your judgments about what you said or did by bringing them out into the light: What are you saying to

yourself? Examples: "I'm such an idiot!" "I'll never get it." "Why can't I just think fast enough!" "I should have done X."

Note: We educate ourselves through guilt, shame and other less-than-fun tactics. We can notice this by our feelings of anger or guilt. Words we often use in the process of judging or shaming are almost always some form of "should" or "shouldn't". These words deny choice and disconnect us from ourselves.

3) Look beneath those judgments to see what need is at their root. What unmet need of yours is expressed by the judgment? (care, consideration). Also, what need of yours was not met by the way you behaved? (respect, connection, etc.)

4) Compassionate Mourning: Meditate on the energy of each need, not the absence of it – what it means to you, why it's so important to you, how you yearn to experience that. If you feel a sweet pain, that is *you* connecting with your need – pain stimulated by past actions which you now regret. Regret can help us learn from what we have done *without* blaming or hating ourselves.

5) Write down what you might say. It might be, "When I behaved in that way (did, said etc.), I didn't meet my need for _____ (care, consideration, etc.), and I know that had an impact on you, and so it's really important to me. Now that I understand this, I would like to deal with it differently in the future, in a way that is more in alignment with my values and creates more_____ (partnership, integrity, etc.).

PRACTICE 2

Restoration – After you are comfortable that you have completed Practice 1, consider contacting the other person and sharing your regret.

> *Note: This is a very challenging process, and requires us to be prepared to empathize with the person's pain, if expressed. We may be tempted to defend or explain our actions. Chances are, our explanations won't be received – just empathize.*
>
> *This is big stuff. If we can't imagine this conversation, chances are we are not ready to approach the person – we need more empathy.*

CHAPTER 24

THE CONCEPT

HEARING NO WITH COMPASSION

A No to Anything Is a Yes to Something

In earlier chapters, we have discussed ideas and practices that help us understand our relationship to the word *no* (see Chapters 13 and 16).

Many of us hold beliefs about *no* that can make it difficult, even devastating, to hear that word. We may believe it means, "I don't matter." Or that it means, "You don't love me." Or, "I'm not good enough." (See Chapter 18).

It can also be easy to believe that "My needs will never be met" – especially when we confuse our needs with the strategies we use to meet them. We think that *no* to our *strategy* means *no* to our *needs* – that *no* means our needs *cannot* or *will not* be met.

Compassionate thinking gives us a way to establish a new perspective and a new relationship with *no*.

HOW CAN NO MEAN YES?

Let's think about that. All the way back in Chapter 1, we learned the first basic concept of *compassionate living* – everything we do, we do in an attempt to meet a need (or needs). And everything anyone else does is the same – an attempt to meet a need (or needs). This can be hard to remember, or even believe, when we are awash in disappointment over hearing a *no* when we were really hoping to hear a *yes*.

That said, we have the option (and hopefully the skill) to perceive *no* as an attempt to meet a need (or needs) – as a *yes* to needs, to life. For example, if my friend says, "Hey Thom, do you want to go out to a movie tonight?" and I say "no," what might I being saying "yes" to? Perhaps rest (if I'm tired), perhaps consideration (if I already have plans with someone else), perhaps self-care (if I am not feeling well).

If we look at any situation from this perspective, we can see that anyone who is saying "no" is doing it to say "yes" to a need. This, in turn, gives us a better chance to have *compassionate understanding*, to see that we are all simply trying to meet our needs.

When we are grounded in this awareness, we are more likely to understand that when someone says "no" does *not* mean "we don't matter", or "you don't love me", or "I'm not good enough", it simply means that in order for someone to take care of themselves, it makes more sense to them to do something else.

OH, BUT THERE'S MORE

So sure, they're meeting their needs – but what about mine, you ask? This is where our ability to see our strategies (our requests of ourselves or others) as *different* from our needs becomes vital. Remember back in Chapter 4, The Riddle of Mr. and Mrs. Smith? We can see *needs* as *not* being in conflict and understand it's our *strategies* that conflict. With this awareness we are more likely to see other, perhaps slightly or completely different, strategies to meet our needs. When we see life in this way, when we hear "no", it doesn't mean our needs won't be met. It just means that this one strategy isn't going to work very well and it's time to think of a new one.

From Chapter 13:

"When our awareness is on our *need*, not our *strategy*, we can hear "no" without worrying that our need will not be met. Why? There are *ten thousand* ways to meet any need. That is the liberation we can experience by having "needs awareness". For example, when we're focused on one or two strategies, in our minds we see only these limited choices. When we think in terms of needs, a world of opportunity opens to us. A world where we can hear "no" without it meaning our needs will not be met."

This understanding is a key in helping me to hear "no" and contribute to a world where everyone can act from choice – where I can have more understanding and less demand, pressure, and tension, and yes, still have a great chance of meeting my needs.

In the big picture of my life, it has become crystal clear to me that my ability to hear "no", with an awareness of needs, vastly improves my ability to meet my needs and stay in connection with those around me. And this affects how much ease, harmony, choice, and happiness I experience. Big stuff.

IN PRACTICE

A Moving Lesson about No – A Strategy Is Not a Need

About six years ago, I was fortunate enough to think about buying a home of my own. I knew it was not going to be easy, because I wanted to stay within a "commutable" distance to New York City. For this to be financially feasible for me, it meant I was going to have to find a great deal, or buy a "handyman special" or some combination of both.

I searched for months with no luck. It seemed the prices and/or taxes in this area were going to keep me from owning my own home after all.

Then, one day, I came across a house that had just come onto the market. It was a bit of a wreck. Actually it was more like a complete wreck. The thing was, it was within walking distance of the train to New York City and the taxes were affordable. The sale price was over my limit, but I made a super low offer. As it turned out, the owner accepted it.

It seemed to me that I had been blessed, that I had won the lottery. It was the house I was looking for and I got it! I was so relieved and happy that I could hardly contain myself.

As time moved on and we entered the process of the sale, things came up. Practical things like, the boiler didn't work. But this was such a great deal – I figured I was still going to be able to make this work. Then it turned out the septic system was substandard and there was mold growing on the walls. But this was such a great deal – I figured I was still going to be able to make this work.

Then we started on the legal aspects. It turned out the owner was actually in prison, so everything took a bit longer to deal with. It also turned out that there was a tax lien on the house, a foreclosed mortgage, and the survey was out of date. Additionally there was some question about who actually owned the driveway. But this was such a great deal –I figured I was still going to make this work. Over the next seven months, we took care of everything.

We were finally going to close the deal on the next coming Wednesday. That Monday, the owner died. I kid you not. It turned out he had two ex-wives, a daughter and a stepdaughter, all of whom had now just inherited the house. But this was such a great deal – I figured I was still going to make this work. After months of legal work, engineering work, mediation, and several thousand dollars in legal expenses, the deal fell through. I was devastated. I was convinced that this was the only chance I had for my dream of home ownership – gone.

So I got some empathy – then some more – then some more. With some time and self-compassion, I realized that my attachment to this house as "my only strategy" had skewed my connection to my needs. It seemed that buying this house was the *only* way I would be happy. I was confusing my strategies and my needs and, as a result, I could no longer hear "no" about this house.

Eventually, I returned to self-connection. I searched inside me for clarity about the needs I was hoping this house would meet. This gave me a new perspective. I could clearly see that I had confused this house with the needs it was going to contribute to – big, very important needs – like security, effectiveness, purpose, meaning, and peace of mind. When I focused on the importance of these needs (*not* the house), everything changed for me. I was able to let go of the strategy of this house and begin to see new opportunities.

I drew a circle on a map of the New York City area. I started the radius at the location of the house I was so desperately attached to buying. As I looked at my new "circle of opportunity", I found several towns that I hadn't thought of before – places that were just as convenient to the city. With this new awareness, my renewed search began.

Within a few weeks I had found the home I live in today, a beautiful old stone house that needed only a fraction of the work of the original home I was trying to buy. It has a larger lot, lower taxes, and is actually quite a bit larger all around.

At the end of this ordeal, I realized how painful and *life-alienating* it can be when I can't hear "no" – whether it's from another person, from myself, or even a set of circumstances – a painful lesson I will never forget.

PRACTICES

PRACTICE 1

Liberate Yourself – (Review from Chapter 13) – Think of a "no" from someone that you are having a hard time hearing (accepting).

Then, write down what need (or needs) of yours you are trying to meet with the request you're hearing "no" to.

Then, write down 3 to 5 ways you could meet that (or those) need(s) *without* hearing a yes from that person.

PRACTICE 2

Compassionate Understanding – (Review from Chapter 13) – After you complete Practice 1, imagine what need (or needs) the person who is saying "no" is trying to meet by saying "no".

PRACTICE 3

Inventory Your Beliefs about No – Write down a list of beliefs that you have about what *no* means. For example, "I don't matter", or "People don't love me", or "I don't deserve", or "I'm not good enough", and so on. Write them all down.

Then, make a list of needs that are met and needs that are not met by each belief.

After that, try writing down some new beliefs – like, "I value living in a world where people can act from choice", or "A *no* to my request is not about me; it's a way for people to take care of themselves, and

I value that", or "Living in a world where I can hear "no", makes my life more wonderful." Make a list of needs that are met and needs that are not met by these new beliefs.

PRACTICE 4

Requesting Self-Connection – The next time you ask yourself to do something and don't do it (yes, you can say "no" to yourself too), ask yourself, "What need(s) am I trying to meet by asking myself to do this?" Write them down.

Then, ask yourself, "What need(s) am I meeting by not doing this?" With this perspective, see if you can figure out if there's another way you could meet both these sets of needs. Perhaps you could do several things.

Share your process with an empathy buddy. See if you can get empathy or strategies from others. Remember, "If you want to travel far, go with others."

CHAPTER 25

THE CONCEPT

LIVING A LIFE OF COMPASSION

Throughout the book, we have been identifying and learning skills and processes that we can use to create a more compassionate life. Even after learning these skills, one of the greatest challenges I have come across is to *remember* to use them. Most of us are so well practiced in our habitual responses that even if we do develop the skills of compassion, we may not use them (see Chapter 9).

This is where I have found that "stepping out of the box" has been a very important thing for me to do. By doing things that are unfamiliar to me, I have been able to grow (see Chapter 18). By doing this, over time, I have been able to create experiences that would never have happened, have relationships that never would have happened, and ultimately create a life that would have never happened – if I had not stepped out of my familiar zone.

As we approach the halfway mark in the book, I would like to celebrate our intentions and have compassion for how challenging the practices in this book can be. Like any great adventure, sometimes stopping, taking a breather and looking at where we've been, helps us move ahead.

Chapters 1 to 4 address the basic concepts that create a foundation for a compassionate life. Reviewing these initial concepts and practices, even after months of practice, can contribute to even deeper learning. Even Olympic athletes do the same basic exercises they did as children. Even the most experienced and skilled spiritual leaders benefit by remembering their humanity – and the basic ideas that engender compassion:

- We're all trying to enjoy life (meet our needs)

- We're all trying to avoid pain (respond to our feelings)

- We all want to experience love (we're human)

- We have all experienced sadness and despair (we're all vulnerable)

- We are all learning about life (we're all new at this)

These remembrances can keep us inspired and give us the motivation and wherewithal to create moments of compassion and beauty in our lives, sometimes when we least expect it.

IN PRACTICE

THE EXPERIMENT AND THE SANDWICH

A number of years ago, when I was living in Manhattan, I was experiencing a problem I had never faced before. As I walked from place to place throughout the city, I was almost always asked for money – mainly by people who appeared to be homeless. It was painful for me to say "no", because I wanted to help. At the same time, it seemed to me, I would go broke if I gave money to every person who asked for it. So I decided to try a little experiment. I decided that I would give money to anyone who asked for it and see how it turned out.

One summery Saturday night during my experiment, a friend invited me to join her for an art opening on the Lower East Side of the city. As I headed out, I remembered to take eight one-dollar bills to get me there while giving money to the folks who asked for it.

It was one of those nights when there was no difference between indoors and out, a completely still, slightly warm, and gently lit city night. As we approached the building it became clear that this event was no toned down stroll and viewing. This was a party – art everywhere, the music pumping and echoing in the street each time the door opened. As I approached the convergence, I saw people dressed in everything from jeans to tuxedos. Folks were friendly, happy, and relaxed. I had the distinct feeling I was going to have a great time.

As we walked up the stairs, a man wearing a tattered coat and a few days of beard on his face, approached me and asked if I could "spare a dollar or two." I pulled out two of my one-dollar bills and handed them to him. Transfixed on the bills, he thanked me as I continued into the building.

After thirty minutes of meeting, greeting, laughing, and listening to music (which seemed a bit too loud for me by now), I stepped outside for a breather. As I walked out the door and down the steps, the tattered man approached me for a second time and repeated his request. I explained that I had already given him two dollars. He responded, "Oh yeah, I forgot. Thanks."

I walked out to the sidewalk and found a nice spot to lean on the building and watch the world go by. As I leaned and watched, I couldn't help but notice this curious character relentlessly approaching person after person, asking for help and experiencing no results.

He was becoming visibly agitated. As time passed, he was more and more vocal and began to change his tone. Suddenly, he began to yell at a well-dressed young man that was on his way into the gathering. The young man had just declined to give money. "What do you mean 'no thanks'? I'm just asking for a dollar!" The man quickly stepped inside, out of reach. This was getting hard to watch. If things kept escalating, I could easily imagine the police would be involved. I was feeling a deep anxiety growing inside me.

A minute or so later, he looked in my direction and we made eye contact. I lifted my arms and gave a shrug, as if to say, "What can you do?" Suddenly, he walked toward me with a look and pace of determination. My anxiety quickly changed to fear as he approached and I imagined what might happen next.

Now standing directly in front of me, he shrugged his shoulders, arms out, palms up, and with frustration and bewilderment in his voice he spoke. "All these people with money in their pockets, and I'm so hungry. All I want is a sandwich." I just looked at him as we stood in silence, connecting to his predicament and his pain. After a moment I spoke. "It sure would be nice if people would just care a little more." He replied in a noticeably calmer tone. "Yeah… it would."

At that point he seemed to be relaxing. He moved from his position facing me, turned and leaned on the building along side me, facing the street. We just stayed there, suspended in the moment, watching the world go by, as the festive music intermittently and ironically surrounded us. In a voice that now seemed to come from resignation and hopelessness, he went on. "All I want is a sandwich – a sandwich with some lettuce and tomato – and some mayonnaise – and some salt and pepper." I had no words. We just leaned there together. In the moments that followed, I could only think of one thing – how to get my new friend a sandwich. I reached into my pocket and retrieved a ten-dollar bill. I handed it to him and said, "Here, enjoy your sandwich."

As his eyes moved from our exchanging hands to my eyes, his expression went from disbelief, to surprise, to glee. He looked as if he had won the lottery. He leaped toward me and pulled his head to my chest in a hug that almost knocked me off my feet. "Thank you, thank you so much! This is great!" He turned to head down the street, then turned back with an outstretched hand. As we shook hands, he spoke. "Nice to meet you. My name is Thomas." I replied, "Mine too!" We had a laugh and he walked off – to get his sandwich – a sandwich with lettuce and tomato – and mayonnaise and salt and pepper.

As I walked home that night, I realized how incredibly similar we all are. I made myself a promise to remember that. My experiment was a success.

PRACTICES

PRACTICE 1

Review and Renew – Go back to Chapters 1 to 4 and choose two or three practices to repeat.

PRACTICE 2

We Can Inspire One Another – If you do not yet have an empathy buddy, you may want to consider this as a way to create more practice, and ultimately, more integration into daily life. See Appendix F for the link to our Empathy Buddy Forum.

CHAPTER 26

THE CONCEPT

CLARITY ABOUT JUDGMENTS

Moralistic versus Value-Oriented Judgments and Assessments

I n previous chapters we have worked on distinguishing and translating our judgments. To review these ideas you may want to review Chapters 2, 6, and 8.

To add clarity to this process, I have found it helpful to think about judgments in a few different ways. First, it can be easy to think we *shouldn't* judge. I usually have a little chuckle when I find myself thinking this way, mainly because I'm doing *exactly* what I'm thinking I *shouldn't* do. It's kind of like being in a "judgment hall of mirrors", judging my judging. I have come to realize that I will probably always have judgments. As a human, I'm an "Evaluating Machine". That said, I can see many of my judgments as being helpful, even *life-serving*, depending on their nature.

MORALISTIC JUDGMENTS

Moralistic judgments are the *right/wrong, good/bad, should/shouldn't* variety that we have discussed in Chapters 2, 6, and 8. They can be described as beliefs or thoughts that we have – that are not consciously connected to our needs. We often inherit them from our families and cultures. In my experience, judgments like these can make it difficult to stay aware of my needs and the needs of others, especially when I'm upset. When I can recognize these judgments, I can *translate* them – as a way of discerning my needs and values – and return to a more *life-connected* awareness (see Chapter 2).

VALUE-ORIENTED JUDGMENTS

Value-oriented judgments are a different breed of judgment. They are connected to what I want, like, or value. For example, if I said, "I really don't like my neighbor," you might think this is a *moralistic judgment* – but is it? Am I saying there is something wrong with him? Am I saying he should be or act differently? Not really. I'm simply expressing the pain I experience when I'm around him. This is a very important distinction in my pursuit of a more wonderful life. If I want to be able to connect with, and make choices in relation to my feelings (and my needs), I must feel and acknowledge them. If we think we *should* like someone, we run the risk of "shoulding" our-selves into a situation where our wellbeing becomes diminished, and the wonder of life escapes us. We start participating in a *paradigm of moral judgment* and the undistinguished needs stay undistinguished. No fun, no compassion.

I have seen situations where the benefit of *value-oriented judgments* is turned upside down. For example, one time a friend asked me to go out to see a movie. It was a movie I had no interest in at all. I explained to my friend that I really didn't think I would enjoy it and declined her invitation. She responded to my explanation with "You're making a judgment!" – as if I *shouldn't* be expressing what I thought I might like or not like. If I thought I *shouldn't* make that kind of judgment, I could easily see a lot of movies I didn't want to and, for that matter, lose sight of my life in more important ways.

ASSESSMENTS

An *assessment* can be seen as a *cognitive judgment*. As humans, we make *assessments* all the time. If we alienate ourselves from this skill, we can get very confused, even injured. We make *assessments* when we walk across the street. "Is it safe? Are there any cars that might hit me? Can I walk across in time, before the light changes?" I make *assessments* when I look for a parking spot on the street. "Will my car fit there?" I intend to make *assessments* for the rest of my life. It serves me.

INTUITION

There are times when I have a feeling and I cannot make an observation about what is causing it. This can be called *intuition*, although I have learned to think of it as *body wisdom*. My eyes, my brain, and my nervous system all get together and go to work without me. So when I get a feeling like this I can use it as a cue to look around and see what I might be able to bring into my consciousness. This practice has and continues to make my life more wonderful (and saved it a time or two).

GOOD NEWS

Knowing these distinctions about *moral* and *value-oriented judgments*, *assessments*, and *intuition* has helped me fine-tune my practice of compassionate living. They are a way of understanding myself better. By recognizing these distinctly different forms of judgment I can increase my choice, self-care, passion, and compassion.

IN PRACTICE

THE SLEEPOVER

Some years ago, when my sons were in high school and I was starting to practice compassionate living and thinking, my younger son Patrick and I had a conversation that surprised and enlightened me.

It was a Wednesday afternoon, and I was working in my home office when he came in and said, "Dad, a bunch of us were thinking of sleeping over at Matt's house tonight. Are you OK with that?"

My first reaction was agitation and a touch of anger. My thought was, "No. When I was a kid, we never stayed over at our friend's house on a school night." Then I thought a bit deeper, checking in with myself. Why was I feeling angry and closed? I realized it was because I figured that if Patrick stayed out, he wouldn't get his homework done or get the rest he needed. This rubbed up against my thoughts about "being a good father" and "what kids should do". I was a bit agitated and replied, "Pat, I really don't think that's a good idea. I'm going to say no to this one."

At this point in time, I had been studying with Marshall Rosenberg for some time and had shared and modeled much of what I learned. Apparently Patrick was paying attention.

Patrick: So Dad, I'm wondering why you think this is a bad idea.

Me: Well, I'm afraid you're not going to get your homework done, and as your father, I really want to encourage you to do well in school.

Patrick: I think I understand that. You want to be a good father. You might want to know that when we get together like this, we work together and encourage each other to do our work. It's more fun and we end up doing an even better job.

Me: Hmmm – let me think about that. It sounds good, but something isn't sitting right. I think I know. I'd really like to believe you, but it's really a challenge.

Patrick: I get that Dad. How about this – when I get done, I'll fax it to you. We can go over it together. This way you'll know I'm really doing my work.

By that point, I was amazed at how responsive and cooperative Patrick was being. I was a bit confused – truly disarmed. That said, something was still gnawing at me.

Me: You know, Pat, that all sounds really good. But when I check in with myself, something's still bugging me – I'm still concerned that you won't get enough sleep.

Patrick (with a big smile on his face): Oh Dad, you don't have to worry about that! Matt's mother is worse than you are! We will definitely be in bed by ten. I'm sure she'll be happy to give you a call when we're in bed.

Patrick had stayed with me through the entire process. He walked me, step by step, from my judgments, my beliefs, and my assessments, to a place of connection and understanding – on many levels. It was a wonderful lesson for me, and a wonderful experience.

Me: Have a great sleepover. I'll talk to you later.

PRACTICES

PRACTICE 1

Review and Renew – Go back to Chapters 2, 6, and 8 and choose two or three practices to renew.

PRACTICE 2

Create Some Clarity – See if you can remember and write down an example of, 1) a *moralistic judgment* you have, 2) a *value-oriented judgment* you have, and 3) an *assessment* you have. Next, write down:

a) The need(s) that your moralistic judgment is telling you that you value.

b) What need you are attempting to meet by having this judgment.

PRACTICE 3

More Clarity – For each of these judgments write two lists: 1) a list of all the needs that are met by holding this judgment, and 2) a list of those needs not met.

> *Note: I can NOT express in these few words, how powerful this practice can be in creating a more compassionate life.*

CHAPTER 27

THE CONCEPT

CONNECTING TO LIFE-ENERGY

Feelings and needs are like the wind — we can't see them; we can only feel them and see their effects

In previous chapters we have discussed and practiced identifying and naming our feelings and needs. In the early stages of practicing compassionate living, this can be difficult and even confusing. I recall in my "beginning years" that even though I could name my feelings and needs, something fell short. It was the *deeper connection* to those energies that was missing.

When I think of this, it makes perfect sense. For one thing, I (as do many of us) believed that feelings were something to be avoided, something that served no purpose and existed only as a useless source of pain (see Chapter 3). I also believed that having needs was a "bad" thing and that I was being "needy" or "selfish" if I paid attention to them. So when I did identify my needs, it was with a certain tentativeness and sometimes guilt. It occurred to me that regardless of my attitude toward feelings and needs, I had them. Like the weather, they were part of life. Indeed, they *were* life. After all, what do we call someone without needs? Dead. So as long as I am going to have a life, it makes sense to me to understand and embrace it.

FEELING FEELINGS

Although at first, it seemed like feeling my feelings was "wallowing" or "self-pity". Then, it occurred to me that thinking like this was my way of avoiding or judging my feelings (see Chapters 3 and 7). Eventually, with practice, I discovered that feeling my feelings could *activate* my awareness of my needs in a deeper, more effective, and constructive way. This may not make sense at first glance (especially in the light of how most of us have experienced feelings) – although, if you are willing to "go there" and try being "with" your feelings for a while, I suspect you will be pleasantly surprised with what happens. I remember once in our weekly practice group, as a practice together, we all shared 5 minutes simply feeling our feelings (see Chapter 7 exercises). The following week, almost every member of our group had a break through of one sort or another. It was a big week for all of us.

MOURNING

Consciously feeling our feelings inevitably brings us in to a deeper relationship with the needs that give rise to them. If we *shut down* when our needs are not met, we are disconnecting from our life-energy. When we stay connected to our sadness – in the awareness of our needs (when they are unmet) – it's a different experience than feeling sadness while unaware of needs – very different. This process or skill of *mourning* allows us to be more connected to ourselves, to our life-energy, and to others around us when our needs are not met – and let's face it; our needs are not always met.

EMBODIMENT

As I stated earlier, needs are like the wind – we can't really see them. So how can we connect to them? I am aware of three ways.

Remembering – When we remember a time (or times) in our lives when our needs were met, we can connect to the experience of them. We can remember what happened, what it felt like, and how it feels recalling those moments. We can reconnect to the energy of the need.

Appreciating – When we appreciate (or notice) our needs being met in a moment, we can *feel* that need being met. Right now, notice your breathing. Every few seconds, you are having a need met. Place your hand on your heart. Notice the beating and flowing – your body supporting your life – right now.

Imagining – This has been a very powerful practice for me, in terms of my ability to *create a more wonderful life*. When I imagine my needs being met, my mind (my imagination) moves into partnership with my life-energy. When I imagine my needs being met, I naturally think of ways to meet them (i.e. strategies and requests).

PRACTICING ACCESS

Remembering, appreciating, and imagining are things that we can practice. They are like muscles that we can develop over time to give ourselves a deeper and more compassionate experience of all things – from your friends, to your enemies, to your family, to yourself, to a pillow, or a drink of water. This chapter's practices can bring us from *identifying* needs, to a deeper level of *experiencing* and *connecting* to the wisdom of life – a way to be in partnership with life – around you and within you.

IN PRACTICE

THE DEATHS OF JAMIE AND HARPO

I have had two dogs in my life. They both died, as dogs do. The memories of those two deaths live in me quite differently. My first dog, Jamie, died while I was not willing or able to fully feel or take guidance from my feelings. My second dog, Harpo, died while I was more connected to my life-energy.

JAMIE

It was about seventeen years ago when my first dog, Jamie, was reaching the end of her life. She was experiencing renal failure and was in a great deal of pain. I was very busy in my career as a scientist and engineer at the time, so I dropped her off at the vet's office to see what her situation was and what we might do to help her.

When Dr. Finster, our veterinarian, called, I was at my desk in my office. He explained, "She's in a great deal of pain, and I'm not thinking things are going to get better. What would you like to do?"

I knew he was hinting at "putting her out of her misery", and my head started to spin at the thought. I could feel a wave of emotion coming over me. I was panicking, shaking. I felt a deep drive to fight off these feelings. They seemed to simply overwhelm me. In a trembling voice, I spoke. "I guess we should put her to sleep."

He responded. "I believe that would be the humane thing to do. Would you like to come down and be with her?" The very thought of that seemed unbearable. I was terrified at the thought of witnessing my little friend's death. In a fit of fear and panic, I replied. "That's OK. Just go ahead."

To this day, I regret that decision. I understand that it was my relationship to my feelings that made it seem impossible for me to be there for Jamie's final moments. In my fear and panic, I avoided a moment that I can never relive. Although I have compassion for who I was then, I wish I could have been more in harmony with the energies life was offering me in those moments.

HARPO

Six summers ago, my second dog, Harpo, was suffering from a cancerous tumor that had reoccurred after two surgeries.

A few weeks after the second surgery, I brought Harpo in and spoke with our new veterinarian, Dr. Donnelly. "It doesn't look good," he said. As his words landed, I could feel the depth of sadness growing inside me. This was going to be the end of Harpo's life.

Something was different this time. I was not *overcome* by this sadness, I was *awash* in it. It was not my "enemy", or something to be feared, it was a *message*. I had come to love my little companion and teacher. My sadness was a message of love, caring, and companionship.

From this place of sadness and love (not fear, like my last experience with Jamie) I was able to address both my needs and Harpo's. I spoke. "So how long will he live?" Dr. Donnelly replied, "It could be a month, maybe three."

All I could think about was how to get through this in a way that addressed our needs. "So at what point should we think about..." "You'll know," he interrupted, "You'll know."

He was right. For the next several weeks, I watched Harpo lose his vitality. I often cried and held him as he comforted me in my pain. Two months later, Harpo lost the ability to digest food and walk. His eyes told me he was ready. This time I was completely in touch with my feelings, getting guidance about our needs. I knew exactly what to do.

I dialed the phone and through my tearful voice, I stuttered out my request to Dr. Donnelly. "Could you please come here? I don't want Harpo to die in a strange place." A warm voice replied, "Of course."

The next two hours were spent in pure connection with my dying little canine friend. I held him and gently rubbed his little head, as we held eye contact. No fear, just sadness, mourning, and love. When the team came to the house, it was not easy for me – at all. But it was my connection to life, my relationship to this pain that helped me through this incredibly difficult, sad, and loving moment.

With my hands holding his head against mine, we went through his death together. "Here we go, my little man. Here we go." No fear – just deep sadness and love.

If it were not for my ability to relate to my feelings, stay connected to my needs and Harpo's needs, I could not have experienced this incredibly sad and beautiful moment. The memory of that moment brings tears to my eyes and a tightness in my throat as I recall it now, so clearly – a moment that I will never forget or regret – a moment of pure connection to life, even in death.

PRACTICES

PRACTICE 1

Review and Renew – Go back and reread Chapters 3 and 7.

PRACTICE 2

Feel Your Feelings (review from Chapter 7) – Think of a situation in your life where you experience a high level of stimulation or pain. Notice the feeling. Feel the feeling. Stay with this feeling for a few moments. Simply notice and feel this feeling. Stay with it.

You may notice you are judging, avoiding, or backing away from this feeling. Notice what happens, write it down, go back to feeling your feeling. Repeat. Try this for 2 to 5 minutes.

This exercise is an effective way to see how we think about our feelings. It is also an opportunity to deepen our relationship with them (and ourselves) over time. For now, just notice what happens in the coming days.

PRACTICE 3

Embody a Need – You may want to find some quiet space and time for this exercise. Start by going to the Needs List (see Appendix B) and find a need that you would like to experience more "metness" of.

Next, sit back and make yourself comfortable. Close your eyes. Feel your breath.

Now, in your mind's eye, remember a time when that need was met. *Relive* this experience in your mind. Remember where you were, who was there, what was happening… Remember what it felt like… Slow it down… Replay this moment over and over in your mind. Let the feeling of the experience into your body.

Bask in the moment. Bask in the memory – in the feeling.

When you are feeling full or *complete* in this practice, open your eyes. Notice what is happening inside you as you think about this need.

CHAPTER 28

THE CONCEPT

THE LAYERING OF NEEDS

Sometimes needs are strategies for other needs

As we become more aware of our needs, it can be confusing to hold them all in some kind of perspective that works for us.

One concept that has helped me understand my needs is what I call *layering* – the idea that needs can be seen in groups, or batches – an interdependent blend of layers. For example, suppose I've been feeling lonely and I discover that I would like to have more companionship. I might think that since I've connected to my need, all I have to do is make a request (of myself or someone else) and my need will be met.

The only problem is that I'm confused, baffled even. I can't think of a request that would work to accomplish that. So now what? Now I can wonder, "Why am I baffled?" What other need might be part of my situation? Perhaps it's information or clarity. Perhaps I need to find ideas or strategies so that I can meet my need for companionship. So in this situation there is a relationship, or *layering*, of my needs for *companionship* and *information or clarity*.

This *layering* can exist in two ways – deeper needs and *strategic* or *prerequisite needs*.

STRATEGIC NEEDS

Strategic needs are needs that we want to meet *in order to* get another need met. In the example above, *clarity* or *information* might be the *strategic* or *prerequisite needs*.

DEEPER NEEDS

Deeper needs are the needs we are trying to meet by meeting other needs. In the example above, *companionship* is the *deeper need*.

THE LIFE OF NEEDS

You may discover that as you begin to explore this layering of needs, it can be difficult to know if you are aware of a *deeper need* or a *prerequisite need*. A process that I have found helpful in exploring my needs is as follows:

First, as I feel into myself and notice a predominant feeling, I work with this feeling by giving myself empathy or receiving empathy until I can identify the need. I often feel a sense of relaxing when I can figure out what the need is. I may choose to embody or mourn this need to deepen my connection (see Chapter 27).

Next, I ask myself, "What need (or needs) might be met if I meet this need?" This question will direct my awareness to a *deeper need*, if it is alive in me. This may bring a *deeper need* into my awareness – as well as the realization that the first need I became aware of was pointing me *toward* my *deeper need*.

This may change the focus to the *deeper need*, and then to requests to address that need. Sometimes the answer to this question is something like, "I don't really care. All I can think about is how to meet this need I'm already thinking about. I'm so excited!" If this is the case, I'm probably at the deepest need.

If instead, at this point I feel curious, confused, or unsettled, I may ask myself, "What need would I want to meet in order to get this first (deeper) need met?" This question brings my attention to any *prerequisite needs* that may be part of meeting this first need that came into my awareness. I sometimes call this the *surprise need* – a need that was there, that I didn't see at first because I was focused *only* on the *deeper need*.

Two questions can help us *navigate* or understand how our needs are expressing themselves in relation to the events of our lives – in other words, how they are *layered*: "What need (or needs) might be met if I meet this need?" and "What other need could I meet in order to get this first need met?" This helps me figure out what I want to do from the awareness of my needs, and their relationship to each other.

Over and over again, I have learned that going about my life is very different with the guidance of my feelings and the awareness of needs. I have made it a goal to live my life as a partnership between my mind (thoughts), my spirit (my being), and my body (feelings and needs).

The ability to see and navigate the layers of needs takes this partnership to new level.

IN PRACTICE

I LIVE WITH PIGS

In my practice group, one night, I had the opportunity to work with a colleague; giving her empathy about some pain she was experiencing at home. The judgment that we were working with was "I live with pigs."

As I listened and she spoke, it became clear that she had a deep desire for order. It was an important and precious part of her life. I remember the sense of relief she experienced as she came to this clarity. We smiled and celebrated the discovery and connection to this profound need.

After a few moments, the smile drifted away from her face and a look of confusion and despair took over. She spoke. "But I still live with pigs!"

Our celebration was moved to the side as we embarked on the *next level* of our exploration of her needs. It soon became clear that without communication, shared understanding, and partnership, the awareness of the need for *order*, by itself, was not going to help much.

When we could see all the *layers* of needs, it wasn't long before she could think of requests that would address her pain (see Chapters 13 and 15) – and that left her with a sense of hope and life got more wonderful.

PRACTICES

PRACTICE 1

Shifting Toward Compassion Redo – First, begin the "Shifting Toward Compassion" exercise in Appendix C. When you are done listing your needs in the first section, review the needs you have listed. As you read each one, ask yourself, "What need (or needs) might be met if I met this need?" (If you can think of any, add them to your list.) Next, ask yourself: "What need (or needs) would I want to meet in order to get this need met?" (If you can think of any, add them to your list.) Then complete the exercise.

Notice how this changes your experience of this exercise. See if you can think of requests that might contribute to your need(s) being met.

PRACTICE 2

Review and Renew – Go back and reread Chapters 3, 7, 13, and 15, and consider reviewing some of the exercises as well.

> *Note: Although we learn about the basics early on it can still take quite some time before we integrate them into our daily life. It really helps to go back and practice.*

CHAPTER 29

THE CONCEPT

SELF-CONNECTION

Being Centered in Our Needs

A challenge that many of us share, in the pursuit of a more compassionate life, is discerning between what we *want –* and *what we want people to do.*

I think of this process as a form of *self-connection.* It calls on us to use our skills to look inward, or *self-empathize,* in order to pull our attention away from our *strategies* and toward our *needs.* Why do this? Put simply, it changes everything. When we can see our experience as coming from something that resides in us (our needs), it empowers us.

For example, if I'm in a conversation with someone and I'm drifting off, I could think that they are "boring". When I think this way, I can easily see myself as a "victim" to the other person's "boringness". From a practical perspective, there really isn't much I can do in this situation. Can I turn them into a "less boring", "more interesting" person? I know whenever I have thought I could change someone or tried to change someone, it generally didn't turn out well – and it certainly wasn't a fun or connecting experience for either of us.

On the other hand, if I can see myself as *feeling bored* or *feeling restless,* then I can start to wonder, "What need of mine is unmet?"

Perhaps it's stimulation, or connection. From this awareness, I have the opportunity to make a request. Perhaps I could excuse myself. Perhaps I could share my experience with the speaker and ask if we could talk about something else. Perhaps I could ask the speaker a question that would bring more connection or stimulation to the moment. In short, when we are aware of our needs, we are far more likely to be able to do something about them.

So why don't we all just become aware of our needs and make requests? The answer for many of us is that we were simply not taught how to do that. Often, we were taught other things that make it difficult to be aware of our needs – things like, "It's not polite to interrupt", or "A good listener never interrupts", or any number of *shoulds* that we have lived by for so many years (see Chapters 9, 18, and 19.)

SELF-EMPATHY OR "WHAT IS THAT?"

Perhaps the most difficult part of the practice of looking inward is *remembering* to do it. With the skills and practices we have shared in this book, we have our tool kit. We just have to open it and use it.

I can honestly say that the simple phrase "What is that?" has changed my life – sometimes many times a day. That simple phrase is my *key* or *cue* to begin my process, to open up my toolbox of skills, to move my awareness to my own experience – my own life-energy – and to change my moment. This is a "rubber meets the road" practice of compassionate living and a key to creating a more wonderful life. It's what we came here to do.

IN PRACTICE

EIGHT CALLS IN THREE HOURS

I was out shopping one day for about three hours. When I got back, I saw eight calls on my caller ID history. They were all from my colleague, Robert.

Seeing so many calls, I immediately called right back (something I didn't often do. I usually waited for some quiet time).

When he answered the phone, I expected him to be upset, angry, or in some state of panic. I spoke. "Is everything OK?" In a calm, pleasant voice, he replied. "Oh, hi Thom. I just wanted to talk to you."

It occurred to me in that moment, Robert hadn't called eight times because he was upset, or thinking I *should* answer him right away. He was simply in touch with his desire to have communication. In *that* awareness, he was acting on his own behalf – not angry at all – not attached to my actions – just connected to his need.

This was a great lesson for me, imagining how most folks would be, in the process of calling eight times in three hours – the frustration, the upset that usually accompanies these acts. In this case, it simply was not there. This was different. This was easy. All he had to do was press a *redial* button – no sweat, no upset – he got his need met for communication – and I learned something I will never forget.

PRACTICES

PRACTICE 1

Learn to Get Your Own Attention – Keep a small journal with you throughout the day. Make 1 to 3 entries per day, at times when you notice you are feeling some form of unfulfilled feeling or pain.

When you notice the feeling, ask yourself, "What is that?" Then write down what just happened (the observation). Was it something that someone did or something someone said? Was it a thought you had?

Either at that time, or later on, write down a word (or words) from the Feelings List that describes your feeling (see Appendix A).

Then, look at the Needs List and see if you can figure out what need(s) your feeling is telling you about (see Appendix B).

Having this level of awareness throughout your day can be a challenge, and you may experience some frustration or surprise in your attempts. Just remember, these feelings (of frustration or surprise) can help you remember to do this – sooner or later.

You will most likely find that the more you do this, the more natural it seems and the more proficient you will become. This process is *you*, getting your own attention – becoming centered in your needs – becoming centered in life.

PRACTICE 2

Take It to the Next Level – After you have completed Practice 1, see if you can think of any requests you can make that would contribute to the need(s) you have identified.

If you're practicing this for the first time, it may feel like things are moving very quickly. It can also feel scary, like you're taking your first solo flight. You are! This is the practice of compassionate living "on the fly".

PRACTICE 3

More Review – Reread Chapters 3 and 4 about *feelings* and *needs*, as well as Chapters 13 and 15 on *requests* and *connection requests*.

CHAPTER 30

THE CONCEPT

ENJOYING PAIN

I love this chapter's concept because it reminds me that pain can be a good thing. At first, the idea that I could enjoy pain seemed absurd or paradoxical to me. Now, as I look back, I can see that pain has always served me, always made my life more wonderful – eventually – and so *ultimately*, I can enjoy it.

PAIN IS PART OF LIFE

I suspect we can all look back and think of times when we have experienced pain. By *pain* I mean anything from a mild *unfulfilled* feeling such as being *irked* to the deepest sense of *devastation*. As we have discussed throughout the book (see Chapters 3 and 27), pain is as much a part of life as breathing itself. And so, our relationship to it can determine how connected or disconnected from our lives we are. If we fear it or try to avoid feeling it, we are literally separating ourselves from our own lives.

WHY WOULD I WANT TO FEEL PAIN?

As we discussed back in Chapter 3, pain can serve as guidance *if* we recognize it and act in *response* to it. For example, suppose I'm talking to my friend in the hallway of my apartment building, and as we are chatting, I lean back against a steam pipe, which has a surface temperature of 240 degrees Fahrenheit (116 C). Would I want to feel that pain? Of course I would! Otherwise, how would I know to stop leaning on it? So yes, I want to feel that pain because it guides me. This concept can be applied to all painful situations. Pain helps me understand what is beneficial for me, and what is not; what works for me, and what doesn't.

When I remember that pain is helping me navigate through life, it changes my relationship to it. Pain becomes my friend, my guide. This is truer than ever for those of us who have learned to recognize pain as information about the "metness" of our needs.

SUFFERING IS OPTIONAL

When I accept the painful experiences of my life as lessons – as life telling me to do something differently – my life inevitably gets more wonderful. I cannot think of a single incident where my pain wasn't trying to tell me something. I can, however, think of plenty of times where I avoided or suppressed my pain, and increased or *prolonged* my situation. This can be seen as (or called) *suffering*. *Suffering* can show up in many forms – staying in a relationship that is not working, staying in a job that is not fulfilling or productive, or eating food that degrades our health. If we are willing to feel and embrace our pain, we can avoid suffering.

SO WHY DON'T WE ALL EMBRACE OUR PAIN RIGHT NOW?

You may remember, back in Chapter 3, we discussed how many of us learned that pain served no purpose but to hurt us. Many of us have a lifetime of well-developed habits of suppressing or avoiding pain – simply because it really didn't serve any purpose for us. Without the ability to connect pain to our *needs* and make *requests*, or set *boundaries*, it really wasn't worth it for us to feel or connect to it. Many of us have learned to use anger and blame toward others – to move our focus from *our* pain and onto something, or someone, else.

OUR NEW CHALLENGE AND OPPORTUNITY

As we practice noticing feelings and connecting them to needs, all feelings, including the painful ones, take on a new and vibrant role in our lives. We can get to a place where there are no "bad" feelings – there are simply feelings, our guides to help us live a more wonderful life. And yes, it can be very challenging to remember that pain is guidance, especially when it is intense and we want to go back to our old habits of suppression, blame, or anger.

As the saying goes, "If you keep doing what you're doing, you'll keep getting what you're getting." *Enjoying pain* reminds us that we can think and live differently.

IN PRACTICE

TEARS AND SMILES

Several years ago, in my weekly practice group, about eight of us were gathered and decided to give empathy to one of our members who was quite angry at her boss. We all sat and listened as she spoke about the "wrong doings" of her manager, how her manager was so mean and thoughtless and heartless. As we continued, each of us silently translated these judgments into the needs she was likely hurting about. An occasional empathy guess brought the focus from her judgments and anger, to her pain – to her deep feelings of sadness and hopelessness.

After some time, as these feelings surfaced, she burst into tears. As this happened, I scanned the room, as I will often do as a facilitator, to check into everyone's experience. Everyone in the room had a loving, compassionate smile on their face. Yes, a smile. It was a beautiful moment for me. In that moment I could see that we were witnessing the unfolding of a life – the shift from anger and judgment to the discovery of and connection to needs – to life. Our group was enjoying her pain. We were seeing and understanding that this was the stuff of a compassionate life coming to visit – and that from this new place of pain, life would become more wonderful.

PRACTICES

Practice 1

Moving from Anger to Deeper Emotions – Think of a situation where you are experiencing anger. Then, check in with yourself – feel into your body. See if you can find some sadness or fear (or other unfulfilled feelings). Feel that feeling for a few moments. Just stay with it.

If you have difficulty with this, you may want to go back to the practices in Chapter 7.

Next, ask yourself what need (or needs) you would like to have met, that are not currently. This may be a good time to connect with your needs through mourning or embodiment (see Chapter 27). Think of 3 ways to get those needs met that do *not* depend on the situation that you started with.

Practice 2

Un-numbing – Keep a small journal next to your bed. When you first wake up in the morning, write down the first feeling or feelings you notice. Do you have any unfulfilled feelings? Even tiny ones? Repeat this exercise until you identify any consistent unfulfilled feeling or feelings you may experience. Then, get or give yourself empathy about these feeling(s). See what you notice, including any requests you might make of yourself or others.

CHAPTER 31

THE CONCEPT

SHIFT VERSUS COMPROMISE

As we integrate our awareness of feelings and needs, we can create an alternative to the old paradigm of *negotiation*, being carried out through *mutual dissatisfaction*. In a world of *right/wrong*, and *should/shouldn't*, the idea of *shift* versus *compromise* is a new ray of light.

SHIFTING

When we experience a *shift*, it is noticeable by the accompanying feelings of compassion, joy, and/or relief. A *shift* happens when we are able to consciously change our understanding or awareness of a particular need, or set of needs, to a new understanding or awareness. I have referred to this earlier in the book as a state of *compassionate understanding*.

Consider the following scenario. You and a friend have a dinner date at eight o'clock. You have set a beautiful table, created a delicious meal, and are now simply waiting for your friend to show. It's eight o'clock, the soufflé is perfectly cooked and the candles are lit.

Now imagine it's eight-fifteen and your friend is still not there. The clock ticks. Now imagine it's eight forty-five and still, nothing.

Imagine how you would feel. Whose needs would you be aware of? What needs would you be aware of? (You might want to write these down.)

Now imagine it's nine o'clock and still no knock on the door, no phone call. The soufflé has fallen, the candles are burned down and the evening seems ruined. How do you think you would feel? What needs would be bubbling up inside you?

Suddenly, at nine-thirty, you hear a knock on the door – It's your friend on crutches, their arm in a cast and bandages wrapped around their head. It turns out, earlier that day your friend was just in a terrible car accident, almost got killed, broke three bones, broke their cell phone, and was just able to make it from the hospital to your place now.

Now, how do you imagine you would feel? Whose needs would you be aware of? What needs would you be aware of? For most of us, our awareness of feelings and needs would change dramatically. That's a *shift*.

We all have the opportunity to create this experience in our lives, in less obvious situations, when we can remember that we are all just trying to meet our needs (see Chapter 1).

With all the mediation work I have done over the past thirteen years, with all the thousands of mediation professionals I have trained, one thing remains abundantly clear. Any truly successful and lasting mediation comes not from compromise; it comes from *shifting*, where there's a new understanding of the needs of all the parties.

COMPROMISING

Compromise is what we end up with when we're not actually considering the needs that are related to our positions or actions. *Compromise, obligation*, doing "the right thing" or doing "what you said you would do" all come from a completely different place than *shifting* does. In *compromise*, we have some resolution perhaps, although not from a place of understanding and addressing everyone's feelings and needs – and so both parties are likely to give up something.

You may have heard the saying that "A good deal is where both parties feel equally dissatisfied." From the first time I heard that saying; I never believed it. And today, after all the work that I've done as a mediator, I'm clear that it's just not true.

Compromise is not something that has to happen – not when we can develop the skills and consciousness to create a more compassionate, understanding, and creative way of being and living.

IN PRACTICE

PATRICK AND THE TATTOO

When my son Patrick was seventeen, I had been studying with Marshall Rosenberg for several years. One Friday evening, Patrick approached me in the kitchen and informed me that he was headed to New York City to get a tattoo, and he wanted my agreement.

To this day, I'm amazed at what occurred in that dialog. It went like this:

Me: Absolutely not.

Patrick: OK Dad, but can we just talk this out a bit?

Me: OK, but I don't imagine anything is going to change.

Patrick: OK. First, could you explain what the difficulty is for you?

Me: Well to start, tattoos are permanent. You may think it's cool now, but what about in ten or twenty years?

Patrick: I get your concern, Dad. I've thought about that myself and that's why I've decided to only use black ink. Black ink tattoos can be removed if I change my mind later.

Me: Hmmmm. Yeah, but what about health issues. With the risks involved with needles carrying disease – I can't even fathom anyone doing that.

Patrick: No doubt, that's a huge consideration. I spoke to my friend Ryan, who just got a tattoo, and he explained that tattoo parlors are licensed by the State – that they are required to use sealed, new needles, and they open them right in front of you. Believe me, Dad. I wouldn't do this if it wasn't safe.

Me: Hmmmm – yeah, but what about the impression you'll make on people? Tattoos might give people the impression you're not the kind of guy you are, that you're a gang member or something.

Patrick: Well, Dad, no offense, but things are different these days from when you were a kid. Tattoos are much more acceptable. They just don't have the same effect they did when you were young.

Me: Hmmmm [...] Well, hmmmm [...] Well...

My understanding was changing. My awareness shifted about my needs regarding Patrick's wellbeing. Where before I thought my needs for shared understanding, contribution, and peace of mind were going to be terribly unmet, in this new moment they were met.

Before, I thought Patrick's needs for safety, choice, and being seen and understood were in jeopardy. Now it occurred to me they were not. I didn't compromise – I *shifted*. Today, Pat has a tatt.

PRACTICES

PRACTICE 1

Moving from Compromise to a Shift – Think of a situation where you think you have to compromise.

Go to the "Shifting Toward Compassion" exercise (see Appendix C), and follow the format of the two "T"s, starting with your observation (as opposed to a quote), and writing down your feelings and needs, and the other person's feelings and needs.

See if you experience a *shift*, or can think of requests you might make (see Chapters 13 and 15).

PRACTICE 2

Deeper Practice – The next time you find yourself in a conflict, see if you can self-empathize and then empathize with the other person.

To do this, you may have to *slow down* (see Chapter 12) to get to your center and be in a position to empathize with the other person and create a dialog.

See if you can get to a place of mutual, compassionate understanding, where you both understand each other's feeling and needs. Then, see if you can think of a way to resolve your conflict without compromise.

Note: Practice 2 requires the agreement of both parties to participate – both parties must want to resolve the conflict, and take mutual responsibility and care to see it through (no small thing). That said, the rewards are almost always worth the time and energy.

CHAPTER 32

THE CONCEPT

STIMULUS VERSUS CAUSE

*People don't cause my pain — my needs cause
my pain — people just stimulate it in me*

By distinguishing the difference between *stimulus* and *cause*, we provide ourselves a way to think about events and situations in a more compassionate and empowering way. It helps us to bring our awareness away from *what someone did to us* and toward *our needs* and how we can create a more wonderful life.

Seriously?

I remember the first time I heard this idea. It seemed as absurd as *enjoying pain*. I could clearly see that, for example, if someone hit me on the head, *they* caused me pain. If someone "stood me up" on a date, *they* caused me pain. And so let me just say right now, yes, we *can* see things in this way. We *can* see that people do cause us pain. The thing is, where does seeing things in that way get us? Disconnection? Probably. Victimhood? Quite probably. Helplessness? Yeah, that too.

Then I realized the distinction between stimulus and cause is not about "what is true" or about "being right" — it is about seeing things in a way that gives me *choice* — choice to be compassionate when people do things that don't work for me, that I don't like — choice to see things in a way that empowers me and encourages me to find ways to make my life more wonderful. In short, when I think about needs, other things like *being right*, or *blaming* someone for what "they did to me" is less important.

CHANGING FOCUS

When we think that someone is causing our pain, several things happen. First, we focus on them, on what they are doing. We become observers, focused on their behavior. When we focus our attention this way it's easy to become more aware of our judgments ("This person should be different.") and less aware of our needs ("We'd like something different."). By shifting our focus to our needs, we are more likely to take care of ourselves, and less likely to disconnect or feel anger toward others.

Here's a riddle for you. Suppose you have a dinner date (a different one from the last chapter). You leave work at exactly five o'clock, rush to the market to pick up your fresh produce – then rush to the wine shop for the perfect bottle of wine, and finally, rush to the train to get home to have everything ready at seven o'clock, as planned. You pull it off and you have the perfect meal waiting at seven sharp. Only one thing – no date.

Your date doesn't show up until eight o'clock. How might you feel? You would probably be frustrated, miffed, and generally angry. Is your date the cause? Did their actions make you angry? You might think so.

But wait! Let's try this again.

Suppose you have the same dinner date. This time, your boss calls you into their office at 4:55, so this time you don't leave work until 5:16. Again, you rush to the market to pick up your fresh produce, then rush to the wine shop for the perfect bottle of wine, and finally, rush to the train to get home to have everything ready at seven o'clock as planned. Only one thing – your train stops in the middle of a tunnel and you're stuck for forty minutes in the dark. Finally, you get home, an hour later than you planned.

You rush to make your meal, listening intently for the buzzer the entire time, dreading the prospect of explaining yourself to your frustrated date. At eight o'clock, just as you finish your preparations, you hear the buzzer. How might you feel now? In this case, I suspect you would probably be grateful and *relieved*.

But wait. Your date did the same thing as in the first scenario. If their actions had caused you to be upset in the first scenario, why not in this one? Your date did the exact same thing! That's right, your needs were met in the second scenario, not in the first.

IN PRACTICE

LUNCH

I have a friend who I like to see every now and then. We usually meet somewhere for lunch. I don't think I can remember a time when he arrived at our lunch date on time. This became a huge source of pain for me. I brought this to his attention on more than one occasion, hoping he would see my pain and start showing up on time. The more he showed up late, the more angry and disconnected I became. This repeating situation was escalating my frustration to the point that I was considering ending our meetings. I was really conflicted and frustrated, because the truth was – I really enjoyed his company and friendship.

So I shifted my focus from his actions to my needs. I purposefully changed my thought from, "He is causing my pain" to "Although his actions are stimulating my pain, my needs are actually causing it."

This new perspective encouraged me to examine my needs. It occurred to me that I was wanting more choice about how I spent my time. When I was sitting around "because he was late", it seemed I was losing my autonomy and effectiveness.

This new focus on my needs helped me solve my problem. I could stop trying to change his behavior, and simply act in a way that allowed me to meet my needs.

So now, I always bring a book or some work to do when we meet for lunch. I order a cup of tea or coffee, relax, and do my thing – needs met. The tension that was caused by my previous belief that he was causing me pain vanished as I met my needs, regardless of his actions. By distinguishing *stimulus* from *cause*, I made both of our lives more wonderful.

PRACTICES

PRACTICE 1

Changing Focus – Think of a situation where you think someone is *causing* you some pain or dissatisfaction. Write down the stimulus (their action or actions).

Next, write down your feelings and needs (the cause). Then, see if you can figure out how your need(s) might be met by changing *your* actions.

PRACTICE 2

Changing Focus Again – Think of a situation where you think you are causing yourself some pain or dissatisfaction. Write down the *stimulus* (your action or actions).

Next, write down your feelings and needs (the cause). Then, see if you can figure out how your need(s) might be met by changing your actions, or making a request of yourself or others (see Chapters 13 and 15).

CHAPTER 33

UNDERSTANDING ANGER: THE SAME MUSIC, A DIFFERENT DANCE

*"People don't make me angry. How
I think makes me angry."*

— *Marshall B. Rosenberg*

Many of us have grown up believing that we become angry because of what others do. Some believe that it is a necessary, natural, and helpful emotion. No doubt, anger *can* and *does* serve us. At times it can save our lives or the lives of others – at other times, perhaps not.

Over the years, as I have studied and developed my relationship to feelings and needs, it has become evident to me that anger is a very special emotion. Unlike other emotions, it is a mixture of feelings and *thoughts* – thoughts that I can choose to focus on or not. By noticing my thoughts and choosing the specific thoughts I would like to pay attention to, I can experience the benefits anger offers, without the tragic and often devastating cost – to myself and to others.

WHAT IS ANGER?

We can look at anger as a combination of a judgment thought and an unmet need (or needs). When you think about it, you can probably identify these two conditions in any situation where you are (or were) angry.

For example, I used to get very angry when I was stuck in traffic. This was often because I had unmet needs for movement, effectiveness, and choice. I also had a judgment thought – that I *should not* be stuck in traffic.

After some practice, whenever I realized this kind of thinking was going on, I was able to change my thoughts so that I would no longer have this miserable experience. You could say I became mindful. I realized the thought that "I should not be stuck in traffic" was not serving me. I realized that although I didn't necessarily like it, I also realized that being stuck in traffic is a perfectly normal and inevitable part of driving a car on roads with other people who often want to go in the same direction I do. Also, inevitably, there will be times when people will bump into each other and have to stop to take care of themselves and their vehicles.

When I thought about it this way, I realized that there was nothing "wrong". This allowed me to turn my attention to my needs. When I paid attention to my needs, I could see I was losing my sense of choice and my needs for movement and effectiveness were clearly unmet.

Now when I am stuck in traffic, I can usually figure out ways to address my unmet needs, or mourn that they will not be as met as I thought they would. I will use the time to reflect on my day, or to catch up on my communications on my cell phone. I may listen to music. And yes, I still do get annoyed every now and then – although a tiny fraction as much.

185

This is a small example, yet the concepts and practices I use can be applied to much larger manifestations too. Thanks to the basic concepts and practices we have studied in this book, we have the working material to create a powerful shift in how we approach and move through our lives and our relationships.

That said, in the realm of compassionate thinking, this is the "Big Leagues". It is an incredibly challenging undertaking and can often take many attempts before we see success. It requires a high state of mindfulness, slowing down, self-empathy, empathy for others, and creativity – and it is possible.

OUR OPPORTUNITY

We all have an opportunity – not to stop getting angry, but to respond and process our anger in a new, more life-serving, and enjoyable way.

This is a profound topic and undertaking. It influences our personal, professional, and political lives. We will be working more with anger as we continue.

IN PRACTICE

A MIRACLE IN PHILLY

A number of years ago, my partner inherited some furniture from her aunt who lived in Philadelphia. After some deliberation, we decided to rent a truck and pick it up ourselves.

My older son and I decided we would handle things and took off for Philly on a Sunday morning. It was a long drive from our home in upstate New York, although, it turned out to be a beautiful sunny day and our spirits were high. We turned the radio on and enjoyed our journey as we listened to the music in our rented truck. Four hours later, we were in downtown Philadelphia. As we ventured into the neighborhood, the streets were becoming narrower and narrower. As we approached our destination, the roads were tiny compared to our sizable moving van.

As I made the final turn down Pearl Street, Collin and I looked at each other with trepidation – as we realized the road was so narrow there was no way to turn around. It seemed that between the narrow lane and the cars that lined the street, to make it to our destination, we had our work cut out for us.

After about a hundred feet, we reached a spot where it was so narrow we had to move at a snail's pace. My son hung his head out of the right side of the truck and I watched the left, as we slowly rolled down the street.

At the narrowest point, I asked him, "Are we good?" He waved his hand back and forth in what occurred to me as "go ahead". As I stepped on the gas, I could hear the crash of shattering glass and the snap of breaking plastic. In that moment, I realized my son's hand gesture meant "no way". We had broken one of the parked car's rear view mirrors completely off.

Realizing what had happened, I pulled the truck onto the sidewalk, to take a look and deal with the situation. As I opened the door, a very large unshaven man seemed to appear out of nowhere. He was furious. He grabbed me by my shirt and pulled me out of the truck and onto the sidewalk. As I struggled to break free of his grip, he dragged me into the street while my son looked on in horror.

He began pounding my face with his fist. A crowd began to form, cheering him on. As he continued the beating, blood was beginning to drip off my brow into my eyes and I was becoming dizzy. It looked as if I was going to be beaten to death right there in front of my son.

In a moment of clarity, I remembered that I had my cell phone in my pocket. I scrambled to regain my balance and ran down the street while dialing 911 (the emergency services number here in the United States), turning and running back toward my son and the truck as I spoke to the operator. The crowd dispersed like a frightened flock of birds as I ran back to the truck and jumped in. My son was there waiting – speechless with terror.

As I looked down to turn the ignition key and make our escape, I realized it was gone – we were trapped. I looked up and noticed the streets were now empty. Suddenly, the neighborhood looked like a ghost town – not a soul in sight.

For fifteen minutes we waited – perhaps the longest fifteen minutes of my life. As we sat, we made our escape plan in the event of my attacker returning. I would run into the street to get his attention, as my son ducked behind a nearby dumpster. I gave him my cell phone and we waited, scanning the abandoned street. Sitting there in the intense silence, I couldn't help but notice the irony of being in this situation on such a beautiful, warm, and sunny day.

Suddenly, a windowless, graffiti covered van skidded to a stop at the end of the street. We readied ourselves for our escape. As the rear doors of the van swung open, our fear turned to shock. Eight police officers, dressed in full protective gear, poured out of the vehicle, and covered the street in military fashion. We watched, wavering between fear and relief. One of the officers gestured with his hand, signaling us to get down and stay in the truck. While two officers stayed behind, the others disappeared down the street. We waited and watched, as this seemingly surreal situation played out.

Five long minutes later, two officers returned with my attacker standing between them in handcuffs. One of the officers explained to me that the car we had hit was owned by this man – in fact, it was the only thing he owned – in fact, he was homeless. The officer continued to explain that the car didn't even run and was not registered or insured. He asked if I wanted to press charges.

I looked over the officer's shoulder at the man who had beaten me. Although it would have seemed natural to respond to his anger with more anger of my own, something completely unexpected happened.

All I could see was his pain. He seemed hopeless, flanked by the two large police officers, as he stared at the ground before him. All I could see was years of misfortune on his face, the pain that he had experienced – and, in that moment, I could clearly understand this man – how seeing his car, his bastion of security and his one physical stake on this planet, being destroyed – had sent him over the edge.

Yes, I was pretty beat up – but I was safe. My son was safe. I would go back to my home and family, and my life would return to normal. My wounds would heal.

As I looked down the street toward this shackled man, something became crystal clear to me. I would refuse to be part of the continuation of his pain and anger – pain that was so great, it spilled over onto me, and anger that was about to make his life even worse.

I told the officer that I wanted to speak with the man they had apprehended. The officer responded with an incredulous look. "No, you don't," he said with conviction. I took a deep breath, looked him straight in the eye and replied. "Yes, I do." After a few seconds, the officer shrugged his shoulders and walked over to my attacker and his captors. After some discussion, all four of them turned and walked toward me. I spoke to my attacker, as he looked down at the sidewalk between us.

"I'm sorry for hitting your car. I have insurance and I'll make sure it gets fixed." He slowly raised his head and we made eye contact for the first time. He studied me for a moment and finally spoke. "I'm sorry I hit you." He raised his cuffed limbs to shake my hand. As the stunned police officers looked on, I reached out, shook his hand, and simply said, "I understand."

As I think back on that day, I realize a cycle of pain was broken, at least for that moment. It could have consumed me and destroyed him. I could have been part of the "locomotive of punitive justice" – depositions, court appearances, testimony, all designed to send this man to jail to be punished. He would have been arrested, prosecuted, imprisoned, and separated from what little freedom and dignity he had left.

Instead, thanks to the clarity I was given in that moment, it was over – no judgment, no punishment, no anger, no hate – a world I want to live in.

My son and I drove off, with a police escort. We got out of the neighborhood, onto the larger roads and in a few minutes our escort dropped away. We just looked at each other in silence as I realized that what had just happened could have been very different for all of us. We both burst into tears – tears of relief, sorrow, and gratitude. We turned the music back on.

PRACTICES

PRACTICE 1

Dismantling Anger – Think of a situation where you are experiencing anger, in any of its forms (annoyance, indignation, outrage, etc.). Write down your observation (see Chapters 6 and 22 for help with this).

Next, write down your judgment thoughts, all of them – thoughts that describe what you might be thinking this person *should* or *shouldn't* be doing, or thoughts about "what is wrong with them".

After that, see if you can identify some other feelings besides anger, like frustration, fear, or sadness, and write them down too.

Next, see if you can identify your unmet needs and write them down as well.

Finally, see if you can figure out how your need(s) might be met by changing your thoughts or actions.

> *Note: This is a wonderful exercise to do with the assistance of an empathy buddy.*

PRACTICE 2

Heavy Lifting – Dismantling Anger and Making Requests – Go through Practice 1. This time, think of a request you might make to begin a dialog with the other person, that you can hear "no" to and still be OK (see Chapters 13 and 15).

> *Hint: If you do actually make a request, starting with a CONNECTION REQUEST usually helps. Understanding what is alive in the other person will make a big difference if you want to experience a connection and communicate clearly and compassionately.*

> *Note: This is VERY challenging work. Approach it with love and care for all involved and be prepared to SLOW DOWN (see Chapter 12 for help with this).*

CHAPTER 34

THE CONCEPT

BEING RESPONSIVE VERSUS RESPONSIBLE

"If you want to be miserable, listen to another person's anger. If you want to be depressed, believe it."

— *Marshall Rosenberg*

As we discussed last chapter, we can see anger in a different light. Instead of seeing it simply as the result of actions or words, we can add the understanding that both needs *and* judgment play a role in its conception. This allows us a new way to relate to and process our own anger and anger in others.

UNHOOKING FROM BEING RESPONSIBLE

Again, as we discussed last chapter, we can see anger as a combination of *unmet needs* and *judgment thinking,* that generates our experience.

This allows us to *unhook* our anger from someone else's actions or words, and allows us to *unhook* ourselves from another's anger. In this process of unhooking, we stop seeing others as being responsible for making us angry. We *also* stop seeing ourselves as responsible for making others angry.

So does that mean if someone "gets angry at us" that we simply say, "That's not my problem. It's your needs and judgments that are your problem so get over it"? As you can imagine, that wouldn't do much in the way of creating a connection.

BEING RESPONSIVE

Although I am not *responsible* for someone's anger, I can be *responsive* to them. In the process of *unhooking* from responsibility, I am less likely to disconnect, shut down, or defend and more likely to care and connect.

When I can take *blame, fault,* and *should have/shouldn't have* thinking out of the equation, I drastically increase the chances of having a more connected, compassionate interaction.

In the realm of *responsible*, I am acting from an awareness *of the other person's reaction or judgment.* In the realm of *responsive*, I'm acting out of an awareness of *my feelings and needs* in relation to the other person's feelings and needs.

THE CHALLENGE

For me, this is an ongoing challenge. When I am facing someone's anger, particularly when my actions are involved, my *habitual mind* can easily slip into *responsible* mode. In this place, I can start thinking in terms of *blame* or *right/wrong*, and if defensiveness takes over, my connection to life diminishes. Especially in *charged* situations – it is a considerable challenge to slow down (see Chapter 12) and shift my thoughts from judgments to the life-energy that is present beneath them.

THE OPPORTUNITY

With practice, we can learn to move from *responsible* to *responsive*. We can transform disconnecting moments into connecting moments. This practice of shifting our awareness from judgment thoughts to an awareness of needs, offers all of us a more connected, compassionate experience in life, often when we need it the most.

IN PRACTICE

A LESSON FROM HARPO

Three years ago, during the weeks when I was moving into my new home, I got a lesson in compassion from my dog Harpo. Completing the move while keeping up with my training and speaking schedule was an exhausting experience for me.

During that time, at the end of a particularly tough drive – at the end of a particularly tough day – at the end of a particularly tough week – I finally arrived home. I could not wait to take a shower and settle into bed for some greatly needed rest. "Ah, home, sweet home", I thought to myself as I walked toward the front door. As I opened the door, a foul yet recognizable stench engulfed my senses.

I carefully stepped into the house to find that Harpo had made a "mistake" on the living room rug. A big mistake – one that continued into the dining room as well – and into the kitchen – and the rear hallway.

I was exhausted, at the end of my energy supply and the last thing I wanted to do was clean every rug on the first floor of my house. At that point, you could say I lost my composure.

I started screaming in a rant of anger at Harpo, "What were you thinking?! How could you do this?! You know better than this!" I went on, yelling and swearing at him.

As I was in the middle of my rant, Harpo walked over and sat himself directly in front of me looking up. His eyes contained what I can only describe as a look of pure concern and love, as if to say, "Are you OK, Thom?"

Suddenly (I mean suddenly), I could feel the anger melting inside me, as Harpo's concern engendered an unexpected, instant connection. I leaned down and rubbed his little head. "Someone's not feeling well."

Harpo was *not* hearing my blame – he was not being *responsible* for my anger. He was simply being *responsive* to my pain, and his desire for my wellbeing. I was in awe of his ability to show such compassion in the midst of my anger.

Although Harpo died that summer, the gift of that moment will stay with me for the rest of my life.

PRACTICES

PRACTICE 1

Moving from Responsible to Responsive – Think of a situation where you have been thinking that you are *responsible* for someone's anger. Write a brief description of the situation.

Next, give yourself – or better yet, receive – empathy for what is alive in you about this situation. After some time and empathy, you may become curious about the other person's experience and want more understanding and connection with them. If so, proceed. If not so, continue receiving empathy (all things in their own time).

Next, see if you can connect with that person's pain. Write down your best understanding of what it might be like for them – what they are experiencing; their feelings; their pain (not their thoughts) – the needs that are unmet, and how important those needs must be to them.

> *Note: You may be thinking, "I don't really know what they're experiencing." I suggest that doesn't stop us from wondering, or even imagining, what it might be like for them. In my experience, it's the process of wondering that brings the compassion and the connection, not a precise depiction.*

This can be a very powerful exercise if we use our skills of slowing down, translating judgments, and seeing and connecting to feelings and needs (embodiment, mourning).

Finally, see if you can imagine any connection requests you might make.

CHAPTER 35

THE CONCEPT

MORE ABOUT ANGER

ACTING ANGRY VERSUS BEING ANGRY VERSUS CONSCIOUSLY FEELING ANGER

ACTING ANGRY

Many of us have learned to express our anger by *acting angry* – by acting it out. This method of expressing anger can be quite effective if we want someone to know we are angry and want to keep the *disconnection* going. That said, it is not an effective way to address needs or *reconnect*. When we are *acting angry*, we are far more likely to create an ambiguous fog of emotion mixed with judgment, and perpetuate a state of disconnection – than we are to re-connect.

Acting angry can take many forms, from "the silent treatment", all the way to the very act of killing another human being.

BEING ANGRY

Being angry is a term that I use to describe a state of *unconscious* anger – when anger is running the show, when it is affecting our brains and our actions, and we are simply being pulled along for the ride. In our *unconscious* state, we are unable to *unpack* or *translate* (self-empathize), and see the deeper causes in our situation (our needs). We are too busy *being angry*.

FEELING ANGER

Feeling anger is the way I describe a *consciously* angry state. When I *feel anger*, I am separate from it – I can observe it inside me. In this state I am far more able to process my anger in a way that is more self-connected and in alignment with my values. When I *feel anger*, I can respond to it by accessing my deeper understanding. When I *feel anger*, I can self-empathize or get empathy from someone, to translate my judgments and to explore the needs that are beneath my anger.

This is a practice of creating peace from violence. Challenging yet profound in its potential.

OUR CHALLENGE AND OPPORTUNITY

Working with anger can be incredibly challenging. On the path to creating a *working relationship* with anger, we will likely experience frustration, feel disheartened, and maybe even hopeless (I know I have many times in this work). That said, for me, the effort has resulted in what I can only describe as a profound shift in how I experience life.

In this stage of our practice we often notice *soft spots* that call for further development and practice of the critical foundational skills discussed earlier in the book. This is where we can start using the "dance steps" we have worked on previously and do more "dancing".

We are called on to reexamine our beliefs (Chapter 18), feel our feelings (Chapters 3 and 7), connect to our needs (Chapter 4), translate our judgments (Chapters 2 and 6), and make requests (Chapters 13 and 15).

I find it incredibly important to remember that it is these skills that give me access to compassionate thought and action. Without them, it just doesn't work.

With practice, perseverance, and love, we can do this.

IN PRACTICE

THE RIDE HOME

One of the most enlightening experiences I have ever had regarding *acting angry* happened one evening when my partner and I were driving home after a party. It was a wonderful party, with good friends and lots of laughs. We both felt quite content as we got into the car to drive home.

As we drove through the darkness, my mind went to work matters. Things at the office were becoming quite challenging for me and as I drove, I became engrossed in my thoughts about the next day – tasks to be done, when to do them, who would do them. It was a classic "Sunday night inner freak-out".

As I discovered later, my partner noticed I had become quiet. And as she noticed my silence, she began to wonder why I had disconnected. Having experienced this before (often with her mother) as a display of anger, she began to believe I was *acting angry*.

As our silent ride continued, she began to get agitated, thinking to herself, "He has no right to be angry." As our journey home went on, so did her thoughts – "How dare he be angry! I didn't say or do anything to deserve this! This is unacceptable!"

Now *she* began to *act angry*. I was getting "the silent treatment" right back – only I didn't know it, as I remained in my web of thoughts about work.

By the time we got home, she was nearing a full rage. I, on the other hand, was just starting to come back to the present moment. As I twisted the key to turn the engine off, I turned, and with a little smile said, "Here we are." She turned toward me with a stare that would have broken the window behind me – had it not hit me directly. She exclaimed, "Screw you!" She hoisted the car door open and stormed into the house.

I sat in the car in silence, stunned as I began to wonder what I did to deserve that. Then I began to get angry, thinking, "I didn't do anything to deserve that!" Slamming the car door behind me, I marched to the house, ready to do battle.

As I stomped toward the door, I was blessed with a moment of consciousness. I realized her anger was not about me. This was coming from some form of pain inside her. Something was going on for her. I just didn't know what it was. As I began to think this way, my anger began to leave me. By the time I got to the house I had decided that instead of doing battle, I was going to find out what was up. I wanted connection, and I was going to call on all my skills to get it.

I stepped into the front hallway where she was intently looking into the closet, clearly not recognizing my presence. I took a deep breath, walked over and quietly asked, "Can we talk for a minute?" She agreed.

After a few minutes of empathic listening, I was able to understand her upset. After that, she was able to understand that my silence was not about her – it was about my worry. We came down from our state of anger and disconnection and began to see each other compassionately again. We were back on track.

A little while later, as we quietly lay in bed, the irony of our spontaneous combustion during the ride home hit me – right in the funny bone. The silence was broken as I started to chuckle. Then, to my surprise, she began to chuckle too. After a few seconds, we were in full-on laughter, as we simultaneously realized the full-on irony of what just happened.

PRACTICES

PRACTICE 1

Noticing – Keep a small journal with you throughout the day. Make 1 to 5 entries per day that include a description of situations where you felt some anger, even a little bit – where you may have been annoyed or miffed or irked. Include any judgment words you were thinking. Just practice noticing. This is the window to *conscious anger*.

PRACTICE 2

Stepping into a Consciousness – Later on, when you have time, sit down with the Needs List and see if you can figure out what need(s) you were in pain about (see Appendix B). Translate your judgment words into need words. As usual, I suggest that you limit the words you use to those on the Needs List. Write them down.

Then, write down any other needs that you notice you were hoping to have met in that situation that were not met. This is a great time to get some help from an empathy partner.

Finally, write down 3 different requests you might make of yourself or others (see Chapters 13 and 15).

CHAPTER 36

THE CONCEPT

SURFING INTENSITY

urfing intensity is a term I like to use to describe the opportunity I have when I encounter someone who is *really* angry and upset. The word *surfing* helps me remember that just because someone's anger is big, deep, and full of energy, I don't have to run from it – or get pulled under or drown in it.

RIDING ON TOP

In Chapters 32 and 34, we discussed "Stimulus Versus Cause" and "Being Responsive, Not Responsible", both based on the idea that it is not specific actions, but our needs that create the foundation of all anger. When I remember that judgment and anger are an expression of unmet needs (and not about me), I am in a position to relate to a person who is experiencing anger in a more compassionate way.

MAKING CONTACT

When a person is experiencing high levels of anger, it can be baffling to figure out where to begin. This act of "making contact" is a "two-parter".

PART 1 - GETTING READY

If I want to connect, the situation calls on me to separate myself from another person's anger, to understand that *it is not about me*, and to be grounded in my desire to create a connection. This calls for some pretty quick self-empathy. If I believe that "I am responsible" for this person's anger, I will be more likely to try to defend myself or judge them, only adding to an already painful situation.

At times when people are highly stimulated, words like "calm down" or "stop that" often show up, particularly when we talk to children, or others that we are accustomed to having power over. In some rare cases we may be able to stop the behavior with these words. That said, we will most likely stay in a state of disconnection, having never addressed the true cause of the situation – their pain, their needs.

CHAIRS

Imagine walking into a room and seeing a man throwing chairs everywhere. You yell, "Stop that!" What do you think will happen? Get ready to duck.

If we want to connect, *surfing intensity* calls for self-empathy and empathy – a willingness to understand what my feelings and needs are, and a readiness to find out about theirs.

PART 2 - GETTING ON THE WAVE

Once I am in touch with my feelings and needs, and once I am clear on my intention to connect, I can "hop on". Much like surfing on a big wave, relating to someone who is angry can be really scary. This is the tricky part – staying grounded in the understanding that this person is in pain, and *not* connecting to their judgment as "the truth". We want to be responsive, *not* responsible.

As you might imagine, saying words like, "So I'm guessing you're feeling anger and needing support", may have little effect in creating connection. Watch out for more chairs! In my experience, people who are really angry are not usually interested in connecting to needs (at first). They usually want to vent – they may want to share their judgments and feelings – way before they have any interest in thinking about needs. This calls on us to *meet them where they are.*

So let's get back to the room of flying chairs. Imagine that I see this person throwing chairs everywhere.

Self-empathy – my thoughts: I'm feeling scared and at the same time I would love to create some harmony – I would love to shift this situation to something else – something that works for everyone.

Empathy: Why is this guy throwing chairs? I'm guessing he is really upset, and he is doing this to express himself, to let people know he is upset. He's in so much pain that it's the only way he can think of doing this right now.

Now I might say to him (in a tone that matches his intensity) "Wow! Somebody must have really pissed you off!" Will I be the target of a flying chair? Maybe. Although, in my experience, chances are – I won't. I will be much more likely to have made *contact*. I'm up on the wave.

Getting to Shore

From this point on, it's all about empathy. In my experience, the ride from anger to connection happens in stages:

1) Moralistic judgments and venting

2) Judgment/anger-related feelings like annoyed, pissed, furious, mad, outraged, livid

3) Should/shouldn't judgments (what should be or should have been done)

4) Non-anger feelings like frustrated, fearful, sad, confused

5) Needs (life-energy, what we would love to experience)

This journey can take several minutes, several hours, or several days. In its most profound manifestation it can last for generations.

OUR OPPORTUNITY

This concept of *surfing intensity* helps me remember that we can all move from anger to connection – eventually. It also reminds me that when I am centered in my awareness of needs, I can be a voice for compassion in my life, for other people, and for the world. This is our challenge and our opportunity.

IN PRACTICE

THE SCREAMING CHURCH LADY

A number of years ago, when I started out teaching compassionate thinking and living, I was asked to offer an introductory training at a local church in New York City.

There were about twenty of us sitting in a circle. I had explained some introductory concepts and people in the room were asking questions that were taking our understanding and cohesiveness as a group in a forward direction. I was beginning to relax and enjoy our gathering.

Then, one of the participants asked me how I thought this work related to Christianity. As I thought about her question, it occurred to me that this could be a subject that would take us on a lengthy "side trip". I was worried that we were going to get into a discussion about Christianity and lose our focus on compassion.

I spoke. "Wow, that is such a big subject. I'm worried about spending so much time that we might not get to finish the workshop. Maybe it would be best if we finish the introduction, and then approach this question later."

As I finished speaking, the woman stood up. In a voice that filled the room, she screamed at the top of her lungs. "How dare you come into my church and talk to me like that! I came to this workshop to get some learning and you just sit there and ignore me? You think you can get away with that?!"

First, I had to get over my disbelief that such a voluminous sound could come out of such a small woman. My ears actually hurt from the intensity of her voice. I then noticed her stare and took a moment to assess my physical safety. Was she going to attack me? I scanned the room for the exit.

Then, I decided to give this my best. This was going to be a true test of my skills. The phrase "baptism by fire" rushed through my head in a moment of irony. From that moment on, my mind and heart became focused in a way I had never experienced before. What happened inside me took place in seconds – split seconds. What happened in the room after that took maybe a minute – one of the longest minutes of my life. It went like this:

Self-Empathy – my thoughts: Wow, I'm really scared. I'm also noticing a sense of inspiration and determination. I'm afraid that this whole meeting is going to fall apart, or that I might be physically harmed and that this could be the end of my training career – or my nose as I know it. And when I think about all my options, I think I'm going to go for connection – walk my talk – here I go.

Silent Empathy – my thoughts: Something is really alive in this woman. She *must* be in some deep pain and needing something – what could it be? Respect? Care? To be seen? Competence?"

I spoke. "So is it that you'd like to experience more care?" She responded. "Don't give me your double-talk! Answer my question!! Who do you think you are?!!"

My thought: "Wow, that didn't work."

I felt like a boxer, huddled in my corner. OK. Wipe off the blood and get back out there! Ding ding!

I tried again, this time raising my voice. "So you think I'm full of it! And you want answers!"

"Yes!!"

"And you'd like some respect and consideration!" I found myself yelling now, matching her intensity. I was *with* her, not humoring or analyzing her.

"Yes!" Her volume was lowering. We were starting to connect.

"And when I said I wanted to deal with this later, that was just totally frustrating." My volume was coming down now too.

"Yes." We were talking now, not yelling.

"I think I understand. Thank you for talking this out with me." I paused before I spoke, letting the connection between us take hold before I spoke again. "I would just ask that you try to understand that I really want to work on this with you *and* I'm really conflicted. I really want this workshop to go smoothly and now I'm really afraid it might not."

Her stare turned to what I believed was a look of understanding, compassion, and maybe a touch of embarrassment. With a nod, she spoke. "OK." She sat down.

"Thank you."

We finished the workshop. It went quite nicely. As the meeting ended and we were talking about our time together, it became clear that many folks in the room thought they had witnessed a miracle. It sure seemed like that to me.

PRACTICES

PRACTICE 1

Your Anger Redo – Think of a situation when you were angry in reaction to something someone did or said, where you would have liked to experience more connection.

Then write down what you were thinking, feeling, and needing, including:

1) Your moralistic judgments (what's "wrong" with them, "self-ish", "inconsiderate", etc.)

2) Your anger-related feelings (like annoyed, pissed, furious, mad, outraged, livid)

3) Your should/shouldn't judgments (what they *should* or *shouldn't* have done)

4) Your non-anger feelings (like frustrated, fearful, sad, confused)

5) Your needs (your own life-energy and what you would love to experience)

PRACTICE 2

Their Anger Redo – Think of a situation when someone was angry in reaction to something you did or said, where you would have liked to experience more connection.

Then write down what you imagine they were thinking, feeling, and needing, including:

1) Their moralistic judgments of me ("selfish", "inconsiderate", etc.)

2) Their anger-related feelings (like annoyed, pissed, furious, mad, outraged, livid)

3) Their should/shouldn't judgments (what I *should* or *shouldn't* have done)

4) Their non-anger feelings (like frustrated, fearful, sad, confused)

5) Their needs (their own life-energy and what they would love to experience)

Finally, write down what you might say to them to create more connection, in light of your inquiry about these thoughts, feelings, and needs.

CHAPTER 37

COMPASSIONATE INTENSITY

EXPRESSING OUR PASSION
AND DRIVE

ompassionate intensity is a term I use to remind myself that I can live in a self-connected and compassionate way, while I experience and express all of the emotional energy my life has to offer. After all, being compassionate *doesn't* mean I don't get upset or feel emotions. It *does* mean I can go through these experiences with less judging and blaming, and more life-connecting thoughts and words.

INTENSE DOESN'T MEAN ANGRY

Many of us have learned to judge ourselves or others when our needs are unmet. When we shift our focus to our pain (and not our judgments), we can express our pain in a way that reflects the intensity of our feelings – without the disconnection that judgment almost always brings. When I focus on my feelings and needs I can scream for *help* as opposed to screaming my *blame or anger*.

COUNTING TO TEN

When I was younger, I was taught to "count to ten" when I got angry. Nobody told me what to do while I was counting, so I would simply get angry ten seconds later. Now when I count to ten I spend that

210

time noticing how I feel, or noticing and translating my judgment thoughts into feelings and needs. Sometimes I need more than ten seconds. Sometimes I need a few hours or days. I have learned that *it's worth the wait* because it allows me to keep my connection with important people in my life. I say fewer things that I regret.

If I want to connect, I am called upon to separate myself from my anger (see Chapter 35). This takes time and skill. It may require me to re-examine my beliefs (see Chapter 18), feel my feelings more deeply and connect them to needs (see Chapters 3 and 7) – to move my awareness from my habitual thoughts to my feelings and needs – my life-energy.

This process gives me new information. It does *not* mean that everything's fine. I may still be in pain and I may want to express that pain. Only *now*, I can use my new awareness to express my intensity differently – in connection to my pain, *not* my judgment.

COMPASSIONATE SCREAMING

Once I am fully in touch with my feelings and needs, and once I am clear on my intention to connect, I can *compassionately* scream. I can yell out, express the full intensity of my experience – while staying grounded in the understanding that I am in pain, and *not* thinking others are *responsible*.

It is intensity *without* the edge. It's yelling for help and understanding, *not* for blaming or judging.

What does *compassionate screaming* sound like? It may sound like "This is driving me nuts!" or "I'm at the end of my rope!" or "I need a break!" or "I can't believe this is happening again!"

These are the words of intense pain for sure, *not* anger – yet still intense.

Our Challenge and Opportunity

The practice of *screaming compassionately* can be very challenging in two ways.

First, I may slip into *judgment mode*. I am so accustomed to *screaming in judgment* that the very act of screaming may invoke my *habitual mind* and I may move my awareness back to a *judgment* perspective. For this reason, I highly recommend rehearsing this practice.

Second, other people may confuse my intensity with judgment. Most of us are so accustomed to hearing people scream in judgment, that we will *hear* judgment and blame, even when it is not there. So when I scream compassionately, I may find myself screaming a reassurance like, "I am *not* blaming you, I am just in a lot of *pain*!" I may even find myself wanting to empathize with the other person's pain about my screaming.

When I'm *screaming compassionately*, I'm expressing myself more fully and authentically in times of intense emotion and need – from a place of self-connection, *not* judgment or blame.

In my experience, this is a challenging practice, to say the least. I'm also grateful for the understanding and connection it has brought into my life. As I've said before, this is a challenge and an opportunity.

IN PRACTICE

I Can't Take This Anymore!

A number of years ago, I was living in partnership with a woman in my apartment in New York City. We had lived together for a year with the understanding that we would see what living together was like, and check in after one year and decide where to go from there.

The year had passed, and although we were not in any form of intense conflict, our energies were not growing together to form the partnership we had hoped for. We decided that we would both be happier if we lived separately. Since she had moved into my apartment, we decided that she would look for a new place and move out in a month or so – that was in April. She began her search.

After a month, she had not found a place. Being a New Yorker myself, I had a lot of understanding about the difficulties involved in finding "the right place". I empathized with myself and with her. Although I wasn't happy about it, I understood. Her search continued.

After another month, she hadn't yet found a place. My frustration was building, although, like I said before, I had a lot of understanding about the difficulties involved. I self-empathized and in my "level headed" way, expressed my frustration and need for movement, as well as my understanding of her difficulties. Her search continued.

It was June and, you guessed it, she still had not found a place. My self-empathy and empathy skills were being stretched to the limit – as I continued to understand and express my feelings and needs and understand hers. I continued expressing my pain in what I considered to be clear, forthright language, and continued to empathize with her as well. Her search continued.

It was September. As huge as my self-empathy muscles had become and as much as my empathy skills were developed, my life was not becoming more wonderful – at all.

Something was missing. I had been studying compassionate living for three years, and although I had heard about the practice of compassionate screaming, I had never done it.

If ever there was a time in my life to scream my pain, this really seemed like it. To be completely transparent, my *choice* to scream didn't seem like much of a choice at the time. I was "blowing up". However, as the moment arrived, I did make the conscious choice to scream my pain, *not* my judgment.

"Look, I understand you're having difficulty, but this is beyond my limit! This is insane! I can't take this anymore! I'm going out of my mind! – I don't know what to do! I've got to move on with my life!"

I remember the look in her eyes. Something had gotten through that was not being expressed in my previous communications. She understood the intensity of my pain.

I felt a sense of relief. Something that wanted to come out of me did. It was intense and it was completely free of judgment. I didn't blame myself or her. I simply expressed the full experience of my pain. This was a deeper form of honesty and expression between us. I had done something that I had never done before – something I didn't even know was possible until that moment. I screamed compassionately.

She moved out three weeks later.

PRACTICES

PRACTICE 1

Scream to Yourself – Think of a situation where you are experiencing some intense feeling and need, where you would like to express this experience in a self-connected way *and* express your intensity.

Next, fully self-empathize. Write down what you are thinking, feeling, and needing, including:

1) If needed - your moralistic judgments (what's "wrong" with them, "selfish", "inconsiderate", etc.)

214

2) If needed - your anger related feelings (like annoyed, pissed, furious, mad, outraged, livid)

3) Your should/shouldn't judgments (what *should* have happened)

4) Your non-anger feelings (like frustrated, fearful, sad, confused)

5) Your needs (your own life-energy and what you would love to experience)

Now go to a mirror. Look yourself in the eye and scream your pain (the feelings and needs you have identified in Steps 4 and 5 above). For example, "I'm just so frustrated! Why can't this just be easier?!" In this exercise, see if you can notice when you are in judging mode versus pain mode. Practice, practice, practice – until you can align your intensity with your heart.

PRACTICE 2

Scream to a Friend – Go through Practice 1, only this time practice with a friend or empathy buddy (preferably who is not directly involved in your pain) and get their feedback. See if they can spot your judgments. If you slip into "judgment mode", try again.

If they see or hear judgments that you are sure you are not holding, practice generating more clarity that you are simply screaming your pain. This may require some empathy.

CHAPTER 38

THE CONCEPT

WORDS AND THOUGHTS THAT FUEL ANGER AND DENY CHOICE

*More about Should, Shouldn't, Should Have,
Shouldn't Have, Have To, Need To*

As we discussed in Chapter 33, anger can be seen as a combination of unmet needs and judgment thoughts. In creating a more compassionate life, I have found it is vital to recognize specific thoughts and words that take me off my path and disconnect me from myself and others.

I have learned that when I recognize these thoughts and words, I can look *underneath* them to the needs I am attempting to meet by thinking or saying them. And this gets me back to a more *life-connected*, compassionate experience.

Of all the thoughts (and the words I associate with them), none have showed themselves to be more pervasive and create more challenge for me than *should* and *shouldn't* and their relatives, *should have, shouldn't have, have to,* and *need to.*

FUELING ANGER

If disconnection and anger were fire, I would list these words as the most effective fuel I know of. When I think back on my most angry and disconnected moments, these words (or thoughts) were involved. When this way of thinking and speaking is replaced by an awareness of needs, anger becomes obsolete.

Ironically, it is easy to think that we *shouldn't* think should/shouldn't thoughts or use these words – that we *should* stop having these thoughts and using these words (see Chapter 8). As we have practiced before, instead of "shouldn'ting" about our "shouldn'ting", we can create a relationship with these thoughts that returns us to more life connection, a *wondering* – "What need am I trying to meet with this thought (or these thoughts)?" and "What is this thought telling me about what I value?"

Over and over again, I find it is by returning to my awareness of needs that I create a chance to connect to my life-energy and my compassion.

DENYING CHOICE

In addition to fueling anger, *should/shouldn't* thinking can limit my access to choice. For example, if I think, "I should exercise", exercise is not a conscious choice. I become the pawn of my thought. Because my desires and needs are not likely in my awareness when I think, "I should exercise", I can easily lose my inspiration and even become resentful.

When I check in with my needs regarding the thought I *should* exercise, I may find that I'm thinking I *should* as an attempt to meet my need for inspiration – for motivating myself. I may also realize that I want to motivate myself to exercise because I want to be healthier and have more energy. By *checking in* with myself, I can connect to my desire to have motivation and my desire for energy and health – to live an inspired, longer, more vital life.

I may also realize that exercise may *not* meet other needs, such as connection, community, and ease, so I may want to acknowledge and act on this too.

By engaging in this inquiry, I transform my experience of *should* to a clearer understanding of myself. This increases my ability to make choices that work for me – based on my needs – not on a thought I may have inherited from my parents or learned through the media.

With more awareness, perhaps I'll realize that I would prefer to do something else to meet these needs, like hiking, or eating different food. I might come to realize that I want to join a community of like-hearted people in a class or club to help me stay inspired and connected. I can stay motivated through my connection to my needs *and* choose to exercise (a very different experience than exercising because I *should*).

OUR CHALLENGE AND OPPORTUNITY

Although it may appear that what I'm sharing here is simple and obvious, I have found that it is the pervasiveness of *should/shouldn't* thinking that presents the challenge.

As we discussed back in Chapter 2 – this is one of the greatest challenges and benefits in the realm of compassionate thinking.

As a child, I was taught to do thousands of things because I *should* - and not do thousands of other things because I *shouldn't* – "say please and thank you", "finish the food on your plate", "do your homework", "go to school", "take your vitamins", "say your prayers", "keep your elbows off the table". The list is virtually endless.

I am particularly challenged in the examination of my *should/ shouldn't* thinking because I find I am like a fish in water, constantly immersed in my *should/shouldn't* thoughts, and thereby, unaware of them.

As a person inspired to create a more compassionate existence, the process of recognizing and translating these thoughts will likely be ongoing until I die. Each discovery is an opportunity to look deeper into myself and choose my actions from a more *life-connected* perspective.

I am grateful for this, because as time passes, I can become more choiceful, compassionate, and connected – and my life will continue to get even more wonderful.

IN PRACTICE

HE SHOULD CALL ME

When my son left for college a few years back, it was the first time he was away from home for an extended period of time. Before that, whenever he was away, he would call in and touch base with me.

As the semester progressed, it seemed he would call me less and less. So I started calling him. Sometimes I would call him three or four times with no response from him. This became a point of contention between us. I wanted him to call, and he very rarely did.

After a while, I became quite angry with him. It got to the point that, even during the few times he did call, I was in a state of annoyance and anger, and we were disconnected. Both of us were unhappy. The situation seemed to be creating a huge rift in our relationship.

At one point, it occurred to me that it was not the situation that was creating the rift. It was my anger – that came from the thought that he *should* be calling me.

When I realized this, I looked into myself to see what feelings and needs were underneath my *should* thinking. I became aware that the *should* was based on my belief (see Chapter 18) that, "If he loved me, he would call." I was wanting more love and connection. I also became aware that I simply missed him (companionship) and was worried, wanting to know he was OK (peace of mind).

Then, I thought back on my college days and remembered how important it was for me to be *my own man*, to have a sense of choice and self-reliance. It occurred to me that my *should* thinking was not only getting in the way of my need for connection, but my need for contribution and acceptance regarding my son's needs for choice and growth.

From this new awareness I realized that nothing was "wrong". It occurred to me that, of course, he still loved me – and although I worried about his wellbeing, I could choose to understand that he was fine, even if he didn't call. In fact, I realized that his not calling was a sign that he was indeed fine.

This recognition of my *should* thinking gave me access to a different perspective that changed the nature of my days and my relationship with my son.

Over and over, this is a perpetual practice – distinguishing and translating my *should/shouldn't* thinking. The more I can do it, the more harmony, connection, and compassion I experience.

PRACTICES

PRACTICE 1

Make Your Life More Wonderful – Think of a situation where you think you "should have" done something.

Write down what you were trying to accomplish by using this should thought. In other words, what need(s) were you trying to meet by using this should thought (inspiration, effectiveness, etc.).

After that, write down what this should thought tells you about yourself – what you value, what is important to you, what you would like to see in the world (self-care, love, self-expression, etc).

Then, write down the need(s) you were meeting by choosing to do something else.

Finally, see if you can think of two different ways to meet all these needs.

CHAPTER 39

THE CONCEPT

AGREEMENTS VERSUS RULES

Yet Another Look at Should and Shouldn't

As part of our initiation into personhood, most of us learned that there were rules – rules that we had to follow or else we would be punished.

As we have discussed before, all forms of thought and behavior are designed to meet needs – including making and living by rules. Rules help us coexist. They help us have clarity, get along, and have shared understanding.

That said, sometimes rules drive us apart. In my pursuit of a life of compassion, I have learned to take a look at the rules in my life and decide if they serve me (and others) to the extent I would like – or not. When I assess the rules in my life this way, I can see if there are other strategies that would achieve the same needs in a more compassionate, connected, and effective way.

THE NATURE OF RULES

Rules, by definition, are static. In the realm of rules, my actions are expected to conform to the rules. In some cases, I find this very helpful and life-serving. For example, I'm happy that we all stop at red lights and go on green lights. This helps to protect my safety and contributes to harmony and cooperation. So when I look at traffic rules through the lens of my needs, it occurs to me that they work for me and for those around me.

In other cases, it occurs to me that this static nature of rules can work in ways that do not contribute to my needs or those of the people around me. For example, we have a rule in New York (as in many places) that if someone takes something that does not belong to them, they are punished by being sent to jail or prison. To the extent that this rule may discourage people from taking my things, I can see that it meets needs for me – to some degree. Additionally, when I think about people who are in so much pain (or so hopeless) that they would take my possessions no matter what – keeping them in prison meets *some* needs for security that might otherwise be unmet.

That said, there are *other* needs of mine this rule doesn't contribute to.

Rules Can Deny Choice and Needs

Through all my years, I have never seen someone take something that wasn't theirs unless they were in pain or mistaken. I have never met a person who acted in a way that was contrary to someone else's needs, unless it was the best action they could think of at the time.

When I see things this way, it occurs to me that the rules we have created about *stealing* and *punishment* do not match my values for care, understanding, or effectiveness, compared to other ideas.

As we discussed in Chapter 17, the idea of restorative justice affords a new way to work with people who have broken the law. It provides ways for them to meet their needs that are less costly to themselves and those around them, as an alternative to jail or prison.

For example, the court may offer an opportunity to learn employment skills, such as cooking, carpentry, or computer skills – a way to give them hope. This form of justice matches my values for care and compassion, and is likely to contribute to my safety too, because employed, hopeful people are less likely to want to take my things.

AGREEMENTS

Agreements, as I like to think of them, are when we come to a shared understanding about certain actions, in order to meet needs. In this definition, we can change this same understanding as the circumstances and the "metness" of our needs change.

This definition of agreements "raises the bar" for understanding and calls on us to *connect* before we *correct* – to understand the needs behind agreements, and direct our attention and actions based on these needs – instead of focusing on a static rule.

The higher our awareness of needs, the more likely we are to be able to serve the needs at hand, as opposed to serving a rule.

IN PRACTICE

MOVING FROM "THE RULES" TO "NEEDS"

When I became a certified trainer with The Center for Nonviolent Communication (CNVC), I signed an agreement that all trainers sign. It stated I would contact local certified trainers before I offered a training in an area where they worked or lived. This was intended to support a level of partnership and consideration.

As a certified trainer in New York City, I expected that I would hear from the many trainers who came to New York from around the country. I looked forward to the shared understanding, partnership, and joy that I imagined I would experience.

As time went on, I received numerous mass email advertisements from trainers who were coming to New York to offer trainings. Over a four-year period, more than ten trainers offered trainings here. Of those trainers, one contacted me.

As you might imagine, I became frustrated, disappointed, and ultimately hopeless. I was becoming disillusioned about this community I had become a member of.

At one point, I was considering leaving the community in a fit of despair. I was miserable in my thought that, "since we had all signed this agreement, and no one was contacting me, there was no integrity in this community."

Then, it occurred to me that I was in *rule mode* and that perhaps I would be better served by thinking in terms of feelings and needs.

In this new awareness, I realized that deep inside I was heartbroken, hoping for a new experience of connection that I just wasn't getting. I was also fixed on the expectation that based on *the rules*, my needs would have been beautifully met. By *centering myself in needs* (see Chapter 29) I became aware of two things.

First, I could act on my needs. I didn't have to depend on *the rules*, or on other people following them, to get my needs met.

Second, in my *rule mode* thinking, I was completely unaware of the needs of the trainers who were not contacting me.

So I started calling the other trainers when I received their advertisements. I shared my confusion and pain, and sought to understand their needs too. I learned that most simply *forgot* the agreement they had made. Others were full of trepidation and overwhelm, imagining they might be asked not to offer their trainings, which brought up great fear that their chance to be on "the big stage" of New York City would be quashed.

This awareness changed my thinking completely. I realized that it was likely that in the moment they read and signed the agreement (which is usually just minutes after becoming certified), it made perfect sense to sign. It also occurred to me that my fellow trainers were always doing the best they could, and the agreement to contact me no longer existed in their minds or seemed doable for them in this new moment.

What was in their consciousness now was different – it was their needs for choice, purpose, self-expression, and security. From this perspective, I became more relaxed and compassionate – more connected to my own values for care and acceptance. I saw my colleagues as people who were simply trying to meet their needs and avoid pain, just like me.

Although I still experience pain regarding this situation, which is ongoing, I now choose to mourn. And in this mourning, I connect to the needs for community, support, and partnership that I love so much. In this awareness, I am empowered to get these needs met, without depending on rules – I can make requests (see Chapters 13 and 15). My hopelessness is diminished and so is my desire to *escape* or *quit*.

Adhering to *rules* and *rules themselves* becomes less important compared to the needs they meet or don't meet. Time after time, when I can bring my attention to the needs in a situation (not simply *the rules*) I become more compassionate, and usually, I can think of something I've never thought of before.

PRACTICES

PRACTICE 1

Rule Redo – Think of a situation where you are following a rule, or expecting someone else to follow a rule, and you are experiencing some pain.

Next, write down the need(s) you are trying to meet with this rule (safety, effectiveness, etc.).

After that, write down what need(s) are not met by this rule or by adhering to it (choice, self-expression, etc.).

Finally, check in with yourself to see if you can think of different ways to meet all these needs – perhaps by eliminating this rule, or changing it to an agreement through a dialog or self-empathy.

PRACTICE 2

Agreement Redo – Think of a situation where you are keeping an agreement, or expecting someone else to keep an agreement, and you are experiencing some pain.

Next, write down the need(s) you are trying to meet with this agreement (partnership, care, etc.).

After that, write down what need(s) are not met by this agreement or by adhering to it (ease, self-care, etc.).

Then, see if you can think of ways to change this agreement to meet all these needs.

Finally, if you think you are ready, speak with the person you have this agreement with. See if you can create a deeper understanding of everyone's needs and come to a new agreement that considers and meets more needs.

CHAPTER 40

THE ART OF MOURNING

BEING DEVASTATED, NOT DEPRESSED

As we discussed in Chapter 27, feeling our feelings can *activate* our awareness of needs in a deeper way. If we *shut down* during the times when our needs are not met, we disconnect from our life-energy. This can leave us like a ship at sea, without a compass – no guidance, no way to find a direction – depressed.

WHAT IS MOURNING?

We could say that mourning is a *conscious* way to experience the "unmetness" of our needs. We can see mourning as a *process* in which two things are happening. First, we are feeling our pain – the guidance life offers us during "hard times" (see Chapter 30). Secondly, when we are *consciously* mourning, we are connecting to the need that is unmet – we are recognizing the importance and the value that need has for us.

Throughout this book, we have practiced feeling our feelings and connecting them to needs. With these skills, we can create a different experience in the face of unmet needs – one where we connect. This is very different than disconnecting or floundering or wallowing.

When I experience my needs in a more conscious way (even in their absence), I can keep my connection to life and live in that *aliveness*. This allows me to live life "head on", without denying it, fighting it, or retreating from it.

DEVASTATED

When I feel wistful, sad, or even devastated, I am connected to the guidance life is offering me. This is not to say that I can always just simply say, "Oh boy! I'm getting guidance. Whoopee!" Working with feelings as intense as *devastation* is a skill that I will continually develop over time.

Also, there may be times in my life when a certain *numbness* can protect me from the full extent to which my pain might express itself – like when I hit my thumb with a hammer or when someone I dearly love dies. In these times, my psyche presents bits and pieces of pain – as I become ready for it. This is why, often, mourning takes time, even when I'm open to it.

DEPRESSED

When I think back on the most disconnected and depressed times of my life, I can see that they occurred when I was unable or unwilling to experience the life-energy that was trying to express itself in me. I was experiencing loss without experiencing the feelings that were trying to tell me about it – the feelings that might connect me to the needs that were so painfully unmet.

In these times I often turned to *should* and *shouldn't* thoughts (see Chapter 38). These thoughts contributed to anger (both toward myself and others) and confusion. This left me disconnected from my internal guidance and kept me off my path to a more wonderful life.

OUR OPPORTUNITY

The practice of *consciously mourning* offers us a way to experience these moments differently. We can feel into the experiences we have when things don't go as we would like. We can feel our feelings of loss and sadness – honor them, and even *welcome* them. In this practice of mourning, we create a deeper connection to the need(s) that our feelings are telling us about. And this creates a path to make life more wonderful.

IN PRACTICE

A TALE OF TWO BREAKUPS

To illustrate how we can become depressed versus what else can happen when we consciously mourn, I would like to offer you these accounts of two different times in my life when I left a relationship.

A DEPRESSING EXPERIENCE - TALE ONE

As a young man of twenty, well before I had begun to follow my path to compassionate living, I began a relationship with a woman I loved very deeply. We lived together for several years, working to build a life together. During that time, it became more and more difficult for us to get along on a day-to-day basis. After a point, although we loved each other, we really didn't *like* being together – the struggle to get along was painful and exhausting.

Neither of us had the tools or skills to understand or deal with our problems – neither did the couples counselors, therapists, or clergy we turned to. After four years of unprocessed pain, we split up.

The year that followed that breakup was perhaps one of the worst years of my life. I was empty and confused, trying to understand what happened and never getting an answer. I was lonely and hopeless, yearning to experience a sense of meaning, companionship, and partnership, all while not even knowing it.

My life was a downward spiral of undistinguished feelings and needs. I was depressed. I became estranged from my friends, my family, and myself. It was a low point in my life that I almost didn't recover from.

A Devastating Experience - Tale Two

The second experience took place some years later. In 1999, I had been married for eleven years. Although my wife and I could coexist, there was a lack of emotional connection and partnership. Our relationship had become that of two roommates, not life partners.

We had spent the last three years of our relationship in marriage counseling. During those years we occasionally experienced brief bits of connection that would leave us soon after they arrived. While she immersed herself in her career, I immersed myself in my business and my relationship with my children. Our relationship was in a coma.

By 2000, we had separated and divorced. After all my hopes, dreams, and effort, I found myself living as a single parent. I was heartbroken – devastated. It was about this time that I began to study with my friend and mentor, Marshall Rosenberg. I was learning to feel my feelings and connect to my needs. Things began to change.

During the following years, I learned to mourn the aspects of life that I had been so deeply missing. It was only through this process that I became acutely aware of the specific needs that I had previously been *unconsciously* yearning for.

Through the conscious processing of my feelings of devastation and sadness, I discovered how starved I had become for a deeper sense of connection, meaning, and purpose in my life. Over time, as I continued to deepen my relationship with my needs, I came to understand that it was my relationship to myself and the divine experience of life that would give me the experience of connection, purpose, and meaning, not a relationship with someone else.

Eventually, I saw that if I was going to be in a relationship that was sustainable and rewarding, I would be much better off choosing it, not depending on it. It occurred to me that from a place of internal happiness and satisfaction I could bring myself as a complete human to a relationship, without depending on it for my happiness. The relationship I wanted would be like icing on a cake, not the cake. This guided me through a wonderful period of personal growth – of learning to be happy on my own.

Through my awareness and actions, I grew to be in that place. My relationship to life became so deeply satisfying unto itself that, for the first time in my adult life, I was truly content without a partner.

And as if by divine design, this self-connection gave me a way to be in a deeply loving relationship – the icing on the cake. I was ready to meet a woman to share in my dreams, not fulfill them.

It was through my process of mourning (which deepened my relationship to feelings and needs) that this clarity came to me.

My ability to consciously mourn changed everything.

PRACTICES

PRACTICE 1

Connecting with Feelings and Needs – Think of a situation in your life where you are experiencing some confusion, disorientation, or hopelessness.

Next, check into your body and focus on what you're feeling. See if you can bring a feeling into clearer awareness. Invite it to the surface. Feel the feeling. Stay with this feeling for a few moments – simply noticing and feeling this feeling. Again, stay with it – at least for 60 seconds, longer if possible.

You may notice you are judging, avoiding, or backing away from this feeling. Acknowledge when this happens – then go back to the feeling. Repeat. Try this for 2 to 5 minutes.

Repeat separately for each feeling you identify.

PRACTICE 2

Embodying Needs – You may want to find some quiet space and time for this practice. Practice this separately with any need that you would like to experience more "metness" of (you may have identified a need after completing Practice 1).

Sit back and make yourself comfortable. Close your eyes. Feel your breath [...] Relax.

Now, in your mind's eye, remember a time when that need was met. *Relive* this experience in your mind. Remember where you were, who was there, what was happening – remember what it felt like. Slow it down. Replay this moment over and over in your mind. Let the feeling of the experience into your body.

Bask in the moment. Bask in the memory – especially in the feeling of it.

When you are feeling full or *complete* in this practice, open your eyes and come back into your space.

CHAPTER 41

THE CONCEPT

ENEMY IMAGES

If It Weren't for Them!

Often, moments of disconnection and anger come from the thought that a particular person or group is responsible for our needs not being met – the idea that if someone else's needs are met, then ours will not be – that they should be different, so our needs can be met.

When we understand that needs are different than strategies or actions, we can create another way of thinking that separates the fulfillment of our needs from the actions of others.

OUR HABITUAL THOUGHTS OF BLAME

When I think about it, it becomes clear to me that blaming has certain benefits. First, it's easy. I have practiced blaming my whole life. I have watched everyone around me blame others for our problems and challenges – from neighbors, to corporations, to political parties, to immigrants, to other countries. By watching the world, I have learned to blame well.

Another benefit is that when I blame someone else for my problems, I don't have to accept responsibility to take care of things myself. I can simply aim my judgment at someone else, see *them* as "the enemy" and I'm "off the hook".

LIFE-SERVING THOUGHTS

As we discussed in Chapter 4, about needs, we can see that needs do not conflict, only our strategies (the ways we try to meet them) conflict. For many of us, this can be difficult to remember because we are so accustomed to thinking in terms of strategies – that we lose sight of needs.

Earlier in this book we learned how we can relate our pain directly to our needs – that we can view our pain as the result of our needs not being met, as opposed to someone else's actions (see Chapter 32). This creates an opportunity to change how we think about all human actions, and ultimately, create a more life-connected, compassionate experience.

REALITY CHECK

As I think about redirecting my awareness to my needs, rather than others' actions, it occurs to me that there will inevitably be situations where someone else's actions so immediately affect me, that I will want to deal with their actions directly – like if someone is coming at me with a knife, or bombing my neighborhood. It would seem impractical to simply say, "Oh well, I'll just do something else." Situations like these call on us to take immediate action. Two things come to mind when I think about this.

First, there are many situations where we perceive that this immediacy exists, when perhaps it doesn't. We often habitually think and act as if there is no other way to respond to a situation when, in fact, there might be – we might have an opportunity to create something new and more life-serving.

Second, in times when there really is this dire need for safety, there is a way to act on it in a *protective* manner. We can forcefully act on behalf of our needs *without* judgment or hatred of others in our hearts (see Chapter 17).

Learning to act in a forceful yet compassionate manner presents a daunting yet beautiful challenge and opportunity for us humans, trying to live on this planet together. It is my hope and dream that we accomplish this as individuals and as a human family.

It's a Choice

There is little doubt in my mind that I could believe, or even argue, that others really are responsible for my needs not being met. Thinking in this way is an option. Although, when I look at the results that this way of thinking has created in my lifetime – all the disconnection, pain, killing, and destruction – I'm sure I would prefer to have another way of seeing things – one that is less likely to create disconnection and hatred and more likely to engender compassion and harmony.

Whether it is a partner blaming their spouse, an employee blaming their boss, a nation blaming another nation, or a race blaming another race, the perpetuation of enemy images doesn't seem to be creating a world I want to live in. It doesn't appear to be meeting needs very well.

The Alternative

As I stated earlier, we can see our needs as separate from the actions of others. We can create another way of thinking. We can choose to see others as simply trying to meet their needs, and yes, in ways that don't work for us.

That said, if we can separate our "enemy" from our unfulfilled needs, we are more likely to think of numerous ways to fulfill these needs. When we do this, we don't need the others to change in order for life to become more wonderful.

IN PRACTICE

IF IT WEREN'T FOR HIM

A number of years ago, I was invited to join a team of trainers who would be responsible for training other trainers.

During my time at our first team meeting, it occurred to me that the form and method that had been developed for this process was contrary to my understanding of what was an effective way of training trainers.

I spent the following months trying to address these concerns with the person who was responsible for coordinating the process. The harder I tried, the worse things seemed to get. The more I shared my understanding and experience, the less this person seemed interested in hearing what I had to say.

At one point I was convinced that this person "was out to get me" and because of this, the entire process was failing – failing to expand the training, and failing to generate qualified trainers. As someone who was thrilled and inspired about the subject of the training and my opportunity to contribute to it, I was devastated. It seemed to me that if this person didn't understand what I had to say, my dreams would be thwarted and the whole world would suffer.

My struggle to get this person to understand me was stimulating tremendous pain in me. I was disheartened and hopeless in my thought that, "If it weren't for him, my needs would be so wonderfully fulfilled – if it weren't for him."

My pain was growing deeper as time passed. Eventually, it occurred to me that I was holding an *enemy image* of this person, and it wasn't doing me – or anyone else – a bit of good.

So I spent some time giving myself empathy and getting empathy from my colleagues. In that process, I discovered that my needs for movement, effectiveness and, most of all, purpose and meaning, were at the root of all this pain. And during this entire time I had been blaming this one person for the fact that these needs were not being fulfilled. I had been stuck in an *enemy image* of this person and distracted from my needs.

After some time and effort, my awareness shifted from this person's actions to my needs. From this new awareness, I realized there were hundreds, if not thousands, of ways for me to fulfill my needs. At that point, I could easily and joyfully join another program or even create my own. I was back on track. My life had become more wonderful.

Through my process, I also came to understand that this person wasn't "out to get me". He was simply trying to meet his needs – doing the best he could. This understanding helped us stay in connection and keep our relationship alive, despite our differences. My compassion and connection returned and I was able to fulfill my dreams. Sweet.

PRACTICE

PRACTICE 1

Changing Your Focus – Think of a situation where you believe that someone is preventing you from getting your need(s) fulfilled – where you believe that if their needs are met, yours won't be.

Next, write down your feeling(s) and the need(s) you would like (or love) to have fulfilled in this situation.

After you have identified the need(s), go to Practice 2 and embody the need(s) you are now aware of.

PRACTICE 2

Embodying Needs (repeated from last chapter) – You may want to find some quiet space and time for this practice. Practice this separately with each need that you would like to experience more "metness" of (from Practice 1).

Sit back and make yourself comfortable. Close your eyes. Feel your breath […] Relax.

Now, in your mind's eye, remember a time when that need was met. Relive this experience in your mind. Remember where you were, who was there, what was happening – remember what it felt like. Slow it down. Replay this moment over and over in your mind. Let the feeling of the experience into your body.

Bask in the moment. Bask in the memory – especially in the feeling of it.

When you are feeling full or *complete* in this practice, open your eyes and come back into your space.

Repeat this exercise with the 3 most important needs you have identified from Practice 1.

PRACTICE 3

Expanding – See if you can imagine 3 ways each of the need(s) that you embodied in Practice 2 could be met. This could include making a request of yourself or others (see Chapters 13 and 15).

CHAPTER 42

THE CONCEPT

POWER WITH VERSUS POWER OVER

How do I want to make a difference in the world?

As we study and practice living a more compassionate life it can be confusing to understand our own power as it relates to the power of others. By power, I mean our ability to create, to make things happen, to make a difference in the world.

I can recall thinking that using my power was "unfair" or "manipulative", and that by using my power I was in conflict with my values for mutuality, care, and acceptance.

With this thinking, I felt lost and frustrated, confused about how I could live out my values for creativity, self-expression, and movement.

Then I realized that throughout most of my life *power* was something that was used *against* or *over* others. It was difficult for me to think about power without associating it with *power over*.

As a student of compassionate living, I have been able to discern another choice when it comes to using my power. By using my power in consort with my awareness of needs, I can act *with* others, without acting *over* them.

Power Over

If we look around us, we can see power is often used in the attempt to control the thoughts and actions of others. In politics, law, media, education, and parenting, we often use power as a means of getting people to do things, whether or not they really want to. And as we have discussed before, this does meet needs (or people wouldn't do it) – including needs for safety, security, efficiency, and shared understanding.

That said, while this mode of using power does meet *some* needs, it does so at a cost. It can contribute to disconnection, resentment, isolation, and alienation. It can readily support us in acting out our *should/shouldn't* thinking and function to deny choice.

The Choice

This is not to say we are going to disavow our power over others in all instances (see Chapter 17). It does mean that we can choose to find new ways to use our power *with* others, especially when the power *over* mode doesn't seem to be working to our satisfaction.

Power With

As practitioners of compassionate thinking and living, we can apply our power, while considering our needs and the needs of others.

In *power with* thinking, we share our power with others, in the awareness of what it is we value. *Power with* thinking calls on us to be aware of why we are doing what we are doing – to check in with our needs and values. It also asks us to understand and trust in the life-energy that lives in others. Although this can be frightening, it also holds the promise of creating a more compassionate and connected world – big stuff.

IN PRACTICE

THE REPORT CARD

Some years ago, as a parent of two teenage sons, I was often presented with challenges that I had never anticipated, let alone knew how to deal with. Many a time, I wished that my children had come with an instruction manual. Since they didn't, it was up to me to learn as I went. One of these learning experiences came in relation to my older son's grades.

Collin was in tenth grade when it became clear we had a problem. He was struggling in school. He was a straight "D" student, and I was quite scared and worried. My response to this situation was to create *structure* for him to follow for the coming marking periods. I created a regime that included a complex series of incentives, benchmarks, punishments, and rewards.

As his father, I pulled out all the stops in my attempt to use my power *over* him. I was determined to "help" him get a better report card. I remember how at odds Collin and I had become during that period – the discipline, the resentment, the disconnection. I remember lamenting that this was simply part of being a parent, the cost of "doing what was right" for my child.

After a full marking period of this "grade improvement program" his new report card came. Collin's grades had gone from straight D's to straight D+'s. I was scared and confused at even higher levels now, not knowing what it would take for things to change.

By this time, I had been studying with my teacher Marshall Rosenberg for a little over a year. I was beginning to develop a respect for the guidance that we all have inside of us, yet often struggle to connect with – our feelings and needs. It seemed my "program" for my son was hardly working at all, as far as his grades were concerned. It was, however, having a tremendous effect on our relationship – we were seriously disconnected.

So I decided to try a new approach. I asked Collin to come into my office for a talk. With his new report card in hand, I spoke. "Collin, if you want good grades, get them. I'll do everything I can to support you. Just let me know. If you don't want good grades, don't get them. They're your grades. It's your choice. Our program is over. You can do whatever you want."

I remember the look of terror in his eyes as I finished speaking. I'm not sure if he was waiting for "the other shoe to drop" or if he was simply afraid of having the responsibility for his grades on his own shoulders.

The weeks passed – as our new arrangement was carried out. My curiosity was torturous as I left him to his own devices.

Finally, the next marking period ended and the new report card came. I was sitting at my desk when my obviously scared son came in to share the news. His grades had plummeted. His report card now included D's *and* F's.

As I read the report card I could feel my heart sinking. Panic began to rise in me. Then, just as I was about to reinstate the *old regime* in a fit of *power over*, something happened. Some other words came from my mouth.

"Wow – it must really be horrible to get a report card like this." Collin, who was sitting on the floor in front of me, looked up and tears came to his eyes. As he began to cry, so did I.

It seemed that Collin's fate was at stake, and we both knew it. It was an experience I had never imagined could have happened so clearly and in such a connected way. My faith in *power with* had somehow

244

transcended my moment of panic, and somewhere inside me I knew this was going to serve us.

During the coming weeks, I noticed a change in Collin's habits. He spent more time in his room doing his homework. He took time on the weekends to pay attention to his assignments. He even asked for help – and, over time, his grades improved. He had gotten in touch with his own power, his own connection to what he wanted – and it worked.

Two years later, Collin graduated an Honor Roll student. And as pleased as I was about that, the deepest reward was knowing that we were both able to access our power and stay in connection – one of the scariest and most valuable things I have ever done as a parent.

> *Note: I shared this story on a parenting Yahoo Group a few years back and two parents reported breakthroughs with their children – one about brushing teeth and the other about potty training.*
>
> *That said, I am not you, and I don't know if this will work in your situation. I am sharing this idea with the hope of giving you a greater sense of choice, if you want it.*

PRACTICES

PRACTICE 1

Power Over Redo – Think of a situation where you have used your power *over* someone.

Next, write down the need(s) you were trying to fulfill in this situation.

Then, write down the need(s) you did not fulfill in this situation.

Next, *embody* all these needs (see Chapter 41). Take your time.

Finally, see if you can imagine a way all or most of these needs might have been met, by making a request (of yourself or others) that would have included the other person's power (see Chapters 13 and 15).

PRACTICE 2

Power With Transformation – Think of situation where you are using your power *over* someone.

Next, write down your feelings, and the need(s) you are trying to fulfill in this situation as well as the need(s) you are not fulfilling in this situation.

Next, *embody* all these needs (see Chapter 41).

Finally, see if you can imagine a new way these needs might be met, by changing your actions or making a request that includes the other person's power (see Chapters 13 and 15).

CHAPTER 43
_____

THE CONCEPT

COMPASSIONATE SELF-DISCIPLINE

Yet another Look at Should/Shouldn't Thinking

I am often asked, "So does living from my feelings and needs mean I do everything that feels good and nothing that doesn't?" My answer is, "Yes and no."

CHOICES BASED ON NEEDS

When I am connected to my needs I may do things that, at first glance, seem unpleasant or contrary to my desires. For example, I love chocolate malts. I also live about a half mile from an ice cream shop. So if I were to follow my initial impulse to have a malt, I would stop and get one every time I left my house, and perhaps another when I returned. So on some level, I may feel a little disappointment when I drive by.

That said, there is a deeper level of self-connection that I experience that prevents me from consuming 736 malts per year – a connection to my desire to be healthy. This desire lives inside me, right next door to my desire to have chocolate malteds. When I check in with myself, I can connect to the different sets of desires (and the needs beneath them) and, in that awareness, make conscious choices.

To take this a step further, with deeper self-empathy, I understand that my need for health is important in order to meet other needs in my life – needs like connection (I want to be around to see my grandchildren and watch my children fulfill their destinies), contribution (I want to be able to look after my parents in their golden years), self-expression (I love to walk, play Frisbee, tennis and golf).

So at times, I may choose not to have a malt, because even though the part of me that wants to have fun and joy would like one, that same part can understand that health is important too. At other times, I may choose to have a malted. This is when my internal dialog helps the part of me that wants health to understand that joy and beauty are important too.

And so I have come to understand that the *strategy* of having malts is something I do want to have in my life sometimes and not at other times (yes *and* no). My self-connection allows me to create a balance in my life – that I can live with (literally and figuratively).

In this connection with myself, I do on occasion *really* enjoy stopping and having a malted. I also enjoy driving by the ice cream shop. As I drive by, I feel grateful and satisfied that I am meeting my need for health.

SHOULD/SHOULDN'T

As we have discussed before, many of us have learned to relate to our actions through the lens of what we *should* or *shouldn't* do. This form of thinking *does not* connect to our needs on any level. In *should/shouldn't* we are prisoners of our thoughts and strangers to our needs. When we live in *should/shouldn't land*, we often feel frustrated, disconnected, and confused (see Chapter 38).

When I remember the times I have acted from the thought of what I should do, it was guilt or shame that was "running the show", not me. In that place, I rarely felt good about my actions. In that place, I could easily deny my needs for fun and beauty *and* the need for health. In *should/shouldn't*, I was unhappy whether I had a malted, or not.

POWER WITH OURSELVES

As practitioners of compassionate thinking and living, we can act powerfully in conjunction with our awareness of our needs. In this mode, we may still do things that are, on some level, unpleasant. In this deeper place of *compassionate self-discipline*, we can choose an action (or actions), even if they initially seem unpleasant (like driving by the ice cream shop or going for a workout). We get to a place where we do, in fact, *enjoy* these actions because we more clearly understand that they are contributing to our needs.

Likewise, we can do things that we enjoy, free from guilt or shame, and enjoy them that much more. In this awareness, life gets more wonderful.

IN PRACTICE

THIRTY POUNDS LATER

About eight years ago, I noticed that my physique was changing. I was gaining weight in a slow yet steady pattern. During that time I decided that I *should* start eating differently, to regain my former shape.

The first few years that followed that decision were incredibly frustrating and painful. I struggled to lose weight by not eating as much.

No matter how hard I tried, I was unable to stay on my diet. I became hopeless and learned to avoid mirrors, scales, and tight fitting clothes.

After three years, my frustration became immense. I was miffed, chagrined, and confused. I decided to ask for some support in the form of empathy from my empathy buddy and my fellow practice group members. In that process, I discovered that my life had become a surreptitious wrestling match of *should/shouldn't* versus *really want to*. For three years, I had been operating without consciously connecting to my life-energy.

In the days that followed my epiphany, I began to discover what was going on inside me (my feelings and needs). This was different from thinking about what I *should* or *shouldn't* be doing – very different.

I came to realize that, although going off my diet met some needs (ease, comfort), I was living in a body that was not reflecting who I was inside (self-expression). For the first time in years, I moved from *should/shouldn't* to deeply connecting to my needs for health, mobility, and self-care. My *compassionate self-discipline* was taking form.

My thoughts shifted from what I *should* and *shouldn't* do, to what I wanted in my life. I began to think more about gaining my health and self-expression and less about losing weight. Instead of *depriving* myself of food, I was giving myself the body that I wanted to be living in.

From this awareness, I began to enjoy counting my calories and eating less food. I was enjoying my journey to health and wellbeing. fifteen weeks and thirty pounds later, I looked in my mirror and saw the power of compassionate self-discipline.

PRACTICES

PRACTICE 1

Compassionate Self-Discipline Redo – Think of a situation where you are using *should/shouldn't* thinking to achieve something in your life. It's helpful to start with something small. It can be something that you are currently doing and not enjoying, or something you have been unsuccessfully trying to achieve.

Then, write down your *should/shouldn't* thought(s).

Next, translate your *should/shouldn't* thoughts (by empathizing with them) to discover the need(s) that you would love to have met.

Next, notice your feelings. See if you can discover any additional needs that these feelings are trying to tell you about. Write them down.

> *Note: This might be a great time to get some help from an empathy partner. Sometimes, two hearts are better than one.*

At this point, you may want to *embody* some or all of these needs (see Chapter 41).

Finally, see if you have a different perspective about your actions, or if there are any requests you would like to make of yourself or others (see Chapters 13 and 15).

CHAPTER 44

THE CONCEPT

HABITUAL AUTHORITY VERSUS LIFE-CONNECTED AUTHORITY

Yet even another Look at Should/Shouldn't Thinking

At this point in the book I imagine it is becoming clearer how much *should/shouldn't* thinking pervades our thoughts and what an important role it plays in how we experience life. For me, I suspect the process of recognizing and rethinking my *should/shouldn't* thoughts will last for the remainder of my days here on earth.

Perhaps this explains why we have addressed this topic so many times and from so many angles. For a *refresher* on *should/shouldn't* thinking, you can review Chapters 2, 8, 26, 33, 38, 39, 40, 41, and 42.

One of the many ways *should/shouldn't* thinking shows itself in our lives is in the concept of *authority*. In compassionate thought and action, we have an opportunity to create a new way of thinking about *authority* that can make life more wonderful. In this new thinking, we create a second definition of authority, distinct from the one most of us grew up with and live with today.

Habitual Authority

Authority is often thought of as something that someone has *over* us or that we have *over* someone else (see Chapter 43). In this way of thinking, people have to do what the person who has the *authority* says. This power is assigned or assumed through our experience, socialization, and our beliefs. This kind of authority is given to parents, teachers, elders, police, managers, therapists and doctors, to name a few.

As in much of the *should/shouldn't* thinking we experience, it is pervasive in our minds and our lives. As a teacher of compassionate thought and communication, I am often in a position to distinguish and refuse this kind of *habitual authority*. I am often asked, "Is this how I should say it?"

My response is often met with surprise and confusion when I say something like, "I try not to tell people what they should say. Would you like to say it that way?"

When we see authority in the habitual *should/shouldn't* way, we deny choice. We believe we (or others) *should* do what the person in authority says, and *not* do what they say we *shouldn't*. Many of us have heard the words, "Because I say so." Most of us can recall the sadness, hopelessness, and frustration we experienced hearing those words.

As in all *should/shouldn't* thought, there is little or no recognition of needs – it is often accompanied by a profound disconnection from the life in us and the life in others. When I think of all the things that have happened on this planet as a result of this type of authority – it is impossible to express the sadness I experience.

LIFE-CONNECTED AUTHORITY

I have discovered another kind of authority – the kind that is choice-fully given to someone. *Life-connected authority* differs from *habitual authority* because it is based on care, trust, and an awareness of needs – as opposed to *should/shouldn't* thinking. With this form of authority, leadership is based on trust and respect, as opposed to fear or assigned power.

Life-connected authority is a kind of authority that I can joyfully strive to embody. This kind of authority calls on me to practice care and act from an understanding of needs. It calls on me to act in a way that builds trust by being *in service to* the people that ask me to lead.

It is the kind of authority practiced by people such as the Dalai Lama, Marshall Rosenberg, and others – where people trust in a connection that is sacred and unyielding. When I think about what has happened on this planet as a result of this kind of authority, my heart is filled with relief, inspiration, and hope.

OUR CHALLENGE AND OPPORTUNITY

As humans who grew up in an environment of *habitual authority*, it can be a tremendous challenge to shift to a more life-connected form of authority and leadership. This is especially true when we are given authority over others. It is easy to imagine that when we are given *habitual authority*, we will *make the world a better place*, we will right the "wrongs" and fix all the things we know are "broken".

Our challenge is to remember that almost every war that has ever been fought was fought with similar intent.

When we move toward *life-connected authority* and leadership, we are asked to trust in the power of life that lives in and guides every human being – a power that is greater than any one person.

Life-connected authority gives us the opportunity to tap into, channel, and flourish in that energy.

IN PRACTICE

A TALE OF TWO AUTHORITIES

When I began teaching compassionate thought and action I was hired to facilitate workshops in several New York hospitals. The purpose of the workshops was to give people a chance to gain a deeper understanding and have a new experience of their own anger and that of those around them.

After several weeks of teaching, I was quite impressed with the "cooperation" that the participants in my workshops displayed. That said, I was feeling a bit uneasy. There was a sense of connection and inspiration that I had experienced in my public workshops that didn't seem to show up in this series of private workshops.

After I noticed this, I decided to check in with the next group of twelve or so participants to find out why they were in the workshop (something I have since learned to do in *every* workshop I facilitate). It turned out that many of the folks were there because their "boss told them" to attend. I began to give the members of the group empathy. In this process it became clear to me that, up to this point, most of them had been silently angry and resentful, and were wanting to experience more choice and self-expression.

Upon discovering this, I found myself quite anxious. I checked in with myself further. I wondered, was this meeting my needs? Did I really want to be part of this situation? It occurred to me that facilitating workshops organized in this way did not contribute to my value for choice or integrity (having my actions match my values).

It also occurred to me that these workshops did not contribute much at all to my values for effectiveness, contribution, and, ultimately, purpose and meaning. I knew that the work we do in compassionate living is very challenging, even when we are dedicated to learning it. In a situation where someone had no genuine interest (and in fact was resentful), it seemed nearly impossible.

So I turned to the class and explained my thought process. I ended by saying, "If you are interested in what I have to say, I invite you to stay and listen. If not, I invite you to leave." The looks I got seemed to range from relief, to puzzlement, to shock, to pure distrust. Several folks chose to leave.

As we resumed the workshop I could feel the connection I had yearned for enter the space. It became clear to me that in my refusal to accept the *habitual authority* assigned to me by the "powers that be", a new kind of *life-connected authority* blossomed. It was by far the most rewarding workshop I had ever done in that institution.

An Ultimately Happy Ending

When I reported the events of the day to the person at the hospital who hired me, she explained that I was "not allowed" to let people leave if they wanted to. That was pretty hard to hear, because at that time, I was being paid enough to be financially secure for the first time in several years.

However, due to my awareness of my values, and my deep desire to live in a world where life is more wonderful, the decision to resign was easy to make. After finishing out my scheduled workshops for the week, I left.

So today, I don't spend my time trying to teach people something they don't want to learn, in a place they don't want to be. Instead,

I teach people who are inspired and living from choice. That's the world I want to live in.

PRACTICES

PRACTICE 1

Transforming Authority – Think of a situation in your life where you have *habitual authority*. It could be in your role as a parent, a teacher, a spouse, a supervisor, or a project leader.

> *Note: The next steps can take quite a bit of time and effort. Getting through them is much easier and more likely to happen with some help from an empathy partner.*

Identify and write down the feelings you have about the situation and the need(s) met, as well as the need(s) that are not being met in this situation.

Next, write down the need(s) you imagine the other person is trying to fulfill in this situation, as well as the need(s) they may not have fulfilled in this situation.

At this point, you may want to *embody* some of these needs (see Chapter 41). Again, this may take some time.

Finally, see if you can imagine new ways these needs might be met, by changing your actions or making requests that consider both your own and the other person's needs (see Chapters 13 and 42).

You may want to see if you can transform any *rules* you are living with into agreements (through dialog or empathy), as a way of meeting more needs (see Chapter 39).

> *Note: Again, this might be a great time to get some help from an empathy partner. Sometimes, two hearts are better than one.*

At this point, you may want to *embody* some or all of these needs (see Chapter 41).

Finally, see if you have a different perspective about your actions, or if there are any requests you would like to make of yourself or others (see Chapters 13 and 15).

CHAPTER 45

THE CONCEPT

COMPASSION AND VULNERABILITY

A s we continue our journey to thinking and living compassionately, we are inevitably called on to rethink some ideas that we have held for most of our lives. It may seem unusual to think of vulnerability as a way of exercising strength or power, yet as I have traveled my path to a more connected and compassionate existence, I have become convinced it is just that.

VULNERABILITY: WEAKNESS OR STRENGTH?

We can think of vulnerability as being susceptible to being hurt, either physically or emotionally – leaving ourselves open to pain, judgment, or criticism. In a world where power is something that is used *over* people, seeing vulnerability as a weakness makes sense (see Chapter 42). In that world, where individuals seek to control and dominate, vulnerability can be seen as an opportunity to advance or leverage power.

In a world where power is something we would like to share, and compassion is what we seek, being vulnerable is a way to advance our connection and understanding, and therefore helps us experience more compassion.

The Power of Vulnerability

Imagine you have done something that is not in harmony with what you value. Perhaps you said something that was intended to hurt somebody, because something that they said stimulated pain in you. In a situation where *power over* or *right/wrong* thinking is running the show, you would be hesitant to recognize or share regret about the pain or disconnection your actions have stimulated. In that situation, sharing your regret would leave you *vulnerable* to the other person's judgment. In that world you could easily be inclined to stay in that disconnected place.

Now imagine you did or said the same thing, only this time you want to re-establish a connection with the other person. By being *vulnerable* and sharing your regret, you create an opportunity for connection and understanding.

Becoming Grounded in Self-Empathy and Self-Compassion

When I think of the things that I have done in my life that *do not* reflect how I would like to act, it helps me to remember that, "Everything I do is an attempt to meet my needs." It's helpful because, in this awareness, I can understand that, although I didn't meet some of my needs (integrity for one), I was doing the best I could in that moment. If I think in this way – as opposed to thinking that I did something *wrong* – I can embrace myself with compassion while simultaneously regretting what I did. I can connect to the needs I would like to fulfill, and the actions I would like to take in the future (see Chapter 23).

Knowing the difference between doing something "wrong" and doing something *we regret*, creates the opportunity to see ourselves and others very differently. When we can stay in the awareness of needs, there is no such thing as a "mean person". There is just someone who was trying to meet their needs as best they could in the moment – in a way that didn't work very well for me (and ultimately them). There is no such thing as an "irresponsible person". There is just someone who was trying to meet their needs as best they could in the moment – in a way that didn't contribute to my needs being met (and possibly theirs).

When we see ourselves and others in this light, *right/wrong* thinking (and other judgments) can be seen as an expression of *pain*, as opposed to something that is "true". From this perspective, we can become *immune* to the disconnecting effects of judgment.

Becoming grounded in this empathic view of the world changes everything. We can see ourselves and others with compassion and still want things to be different. In this consciousness, we don't have to *forgive* ourselves or others, because nobody has done anything "wrong". Instead, we can understand that we would like to experience something different and move toward it with compassion in our hearts.

OUR CHALLENGE

If you're anything like me, the idea of trying to live from a place of vulnerability can be pretty scary. In our attempt to re-frame how we see ourselves and others, we inevitably run the risk of experiencing pain and being the focus of our own and other people's judgment.

However, with practice and experience, we can learn to understand and embrace the power of vulnerability as a step toward the more compassionate life we yearn to have.

IN PRACTICE

I'M A WRECK

About fourteen years ago, when I was just beginning to teach compassionate thought and action, I had the opportunity to teach a class at a university in Binghamton, New York.

For some reason, as the moment to begin my presentation approached, I began to feel nervous. This was unusual for me, as I had given hundreds of presentations in my life. I was perplexed and becoming increasingly nervous as each moment passed. Now I was nervous about being nervous, and on the edge of losing my composure completely. To this day, I don't know why this happened.

By the time I was being introduced, I was a wreck, shaking, and beginning to sweat. As I approached the podium to speak, I realized that in this condition it would be very difficult to engage and connect with the students who had come to hear me speak. I decided to be vulnerable.

I spoke. "Hi everyone. Before we start I would just like to say, I'm a wreck. I started getting nervous a few minutes ago, which hardly ever happens to me, and now I'm shaking like a leaf – I don't really even know why!"

I didn't know what to expect. I put myself on the line because I wanted connection, not knowing if I would be laughed at or judged or thought less of. As I had hoped, my words were received with an instant connection to almost everyone in the room. I find it hard to describe, but the looks and sounds that followed my *confession* were awash with compassion and understanding. The connection went from zero to a hundred and my anxiety was instantly transformed. The crisis was over and I was able to enjoy a fine ninety minutes with my audience of newfound friends.

Although I have this memory to look back on, I also remember other times when things didn't go so well. That said, the connection and compassion that I have experienced in my life by taking the chance to be vulnerable has been precious to me. The beauty of the connection I have experienced in those moments has far outweighed any pain I have experienced from my choices.

PRACTICES

PRACTICE 1

Vulnerability Test Flight – This exercise is challenging. It is recommended that you try the last two steps as a *role-play* with a friend or empathy buddy, at least once (if not 10 times) before you try it for real.

To be clear, steps 1 through 4 are done alone and steps 5 and 6 are the *role-play* parts.

1) Observation – Think of a situation where you did or said something you regret – when you were unable to express yourself in a *vulnerable* way – when you would have liked a deeper connection. Perhaps you were feeling too scared of being judged by yourself or the other person, or you were afraid there would be punishment or retribution.

   Recall the exact action or quote and write it down.

2) Identify Your Self-Judgments – Write down your judgments about what you did. Bring them out into the light. What are you saying to yourself? For example, "I was so mean", "that was so inconsiderate", "I should have done X."

Remember, we often try to educate ourselves through guilt, shame, and other less-than-fun tactics. We can notice this by our feelings of anger or guilt. One of the words we often use in this process is *should*.

3) Translating Judgments to Needs – Look beneath your judgments to see what unmet need of yours is expressed by each judgment (see Chapters 2 and 8). What needs of yours were not met by the way you behaved or by what you said? For example, *respect* or *connection*. Write them down.

4) Self-Compassion – Ask yourself what needs you were trying to meet in the action or words you chose to say or do. Give yourself the gift of *compassionate understanding*. Write a message to yourself like:

"I understand why I did that. I was trying to meet my needs for _____, _____, and _____. And even though I understand that, I would love to meet those needs in a way that is more in alignment with my other needs for _____, _____, and _____."

5) Share Your Vulnerability – Imagine how you might share your vulnerability in light of this understanding.

It might sound like, "I'm feeling a bit scared sharing this with you because I'm afraid of being judged, but I really want to reconnect. When I (did, said etc.), I didn't meet my need for _____ (ex. care, consideration, etc.), and I know that had an impact on you. Now that I understand this, I would like to deal with that differently, in a way that is more in alignment with my values and creates more _____. I'm wondering what goes on for you hearing this?"

6) Empathize – This is when we are the most vulnerable, where we may want to defend or explain our actions. This is the transformative moment when we can – through being grounded in our awareness of needs – empathize with the other person's pain. This is where our strength to be compassionate will be tested. Just empathize and connect.

CHAPTER 46

THE CONCEPT

DEMANDING VERSUS PERSISTING

As we discussed last chapter, on our journey to thinking and living compassionately, we are inevitably challenged to rethink some ideas that we have held for most of our lives. For many of us, one of these challenges comes up when we want to *fight* for our needs or for what we believe in, *and* hold on to our compassion at the same time. In other words, how do we keep the *passion* in *compassion*? How do we keep our power, drive, and desire intact, while thinking and living compassionately?

I am often asked the following question in workshops. "So doesn't paying attention to other people's needs mean that we have to give up on our own?" My answer is usually, "Being compassionate does not mean being a "wimp". It means that we connect with all people's needs, including our own."

As we integrate needs awareness into our bones it can be like learning to juggle. First we become aware of our needs, then others' needs, then back to our needs. With practice, we learn to hold all needs in our consciousness at the same time. This is a skill and a key to compassionate living.

DEMANDING

We can think of *demanding* as the pursuit of a specific strategy, without an awareness of needs. In *demanding* we may want other people to contribute to our needs, without regard to their willingness or their needs. In demanding we get *attached* to a specific person, act, or event. We can no longer hear "no" – from ourselves, from others, or from the circumstances of life (see Chapters 13, 16, and 24).

When I first learned of this concept, I was inclined to use it as a way of "making people wrong". When I believed someone was unaware of my needs I would say things like, "That's a demand!" At first, I was disappointed that they were not instantly curious and wanting to know more about my statement. Over time, I realized that I was using my awareness like a weapon, to judge. It never worked out very well.

That said, I find it extremely helpful to recognize *demands* and think of them as a signal that it would probably be helpful to increase the awareness of needs – mine or someone else's – so we could increase the level of connection and compassion.

COMPASSIONATE PERSISTING

We can think of *compassionate persisting* as acting from an awareness of everyone's needs, while being determined (perhaps even happy, grateful, or inspired) to pursue our own needs.

In *compassionate persisting*, we are open to hearing "no" along the path to the fulfillment of our needs – not because we are willing to let our needs go unmet, but because we want our needs met in a way that *also* considers the needs of others.

We can think of *persisting* as passionate and inspired *requesting* (see Chapters 13 and 24) – a way to pursue our needs in accordance with our respect and care for everyone's needs.

In *persisting*, we understand that there are at least *ten thousand* ways for our needs to be met. This understanding opens up possibilities and a creative process I like to call *the liberation of needs consciousness*.

OUR CHALLENGE

Persisting requires us to remember that our *needs* are different than the *strategies* we choose to meet them. It calls on our ability to self-empathize in times of pain. It calls on us to look beyond our attachments, to see where the energy of life leads us – all while staying connected to the passion *and* compassion in our hearts.

IN PRACTICE

DOGGING FOR HIS NEEDS

About fourteen years ago, when I was living in Manhattan, I began hosting a weekly practice group at my home on the Upper West Side. At the time, my dog Harpo lived with me.

After meeting for a couple of weeks, it became clear to us that having this incredibly cute, soft, and loving creature in the room with us was making it difficult to be present to one another. We agreed that although we all loved Harpo, it would be best if he stayed in the bedroom while we met in the living room.

At our third meeting, as the group was gathering, I sent Harpo to the bedroom in the back of the apartment. He had a rather large vocabulary for a dog, and was also quite accommodating. So when I said, "OK, time to go to the bedroom", he trotted down the hall, into the bedroom. Easy enough.

About thirty seconds later, I noticed two little eyes peering around the corner between the hallway and the living room. They seemed to be saying, "Can I come back now?" My response, "Not now Harpo. Go to the bedroom." Again, Harpo trotted back down the hall. Easy enough.

As we began our *check-in* to start our evening, I couldn't help but notice those two little eyes peeking around the corner again. They seemed to be saying, "How about now?" My response, "Not now Harpo. Go to the bedroom." Once more, he simply trotted back down the hall. This occurred three or four times with the same result until, finally, Harpo figured out it was going to be a while.

I remember feeling some surprise at how easeful my interaction with Harpo felt. As I thought about it, I realized that it was because his repeated visitations were simply how Harpo was making a request for his needs. He never ran into the room, or tried to ignore me. He was genuinely checking in with me, making persistent requests. Each time, he was quite open to my *no*. He was simply trying to find out if this new moment was different than the last.

At the end of the evening I called Harpo in and we had a wonderful time as he made the rounds, saying hello and goodbye to everyone, and then settling down on the couch with me after everyone left.

Although it was a fine evening for the group, with lots of learning, I got the most learning from Harpo that night. He taught me that a *no* can mean *no in this moment*. I can hear "no" as *not now*. And as long as I can hear "no" in this way, I can stay present to my needs and open to – not just other strategies, but other times too. Thanks, once again, to Harpo, my little friend and teacher.

PRACTICES

PRACTICE 1

Liberate Yourself – Think of a *no* that you are, or have been, hearing. It could be from another person, from yourself, or from a circumstance in your life.

Then, write down what need (or needs) of yours you are trying to meet as you are hearing this "no".

Then, write down 10 to 15 other ways you might meet that (or those) need(s) while still hearing that "no".

Practice 2

Persist – Think of at least 2 connection requests (see Chapter 15) that you might make to find out *if* each of the strategies (from Practice 1) *might* work. Yes, this could be a total 30 requests.

> *Note: In persisting, we're fine to hear "no" and can often experience a great sense of choice and abundance as we act on our own behalf, with passion and compassion.*

CHAPTER 47

THE CONCEPT

A COMPASSIONATE VIEW OF TRIGGERS

As we develop and expand our relationship with feelings and needs, it can be confusing, if not confounding, to understand some of the feelings we find ourselves experiencing. At times, the intensity with which we experience these feelings can seem to be *out of balance* or more intense than we expect. In these situations we can easily judge ourselves or others as being "too sensitive" or "over-reacting". Although we can think this way, there is an alternative that I have found to be more connecting, compassionate and, ultimately, more useful.

WHAT HAPPENS WHEN WE EXPERIENCE A TRIGGER?

The term *trigger* is often used to describe events that set off intense feelings. It implies that there is something that has already been set up and is "waiting to happen".

In the case of almost every trigger, what has already happened is that the unmet need we are experiencing has been profoundly and/ or repeatedly unmet in our lives, often during our younger years – so much so, that we have established an intense *habitual* reaction when that need is unmet.

Compassion for the Robot

Back in Chapter 7 we discussed our *being* versus our *robot*. Our *robot* is the part of us that operates from habit. When we are *triggered*, we can think of this as our *robot* taking over and habitually reacting to our unmet need(s). That said, although these reactions may be habitual in their intensity, they are still related to needs. When we can understand that, we can have compassion for our experience —not discount it – and recognize our unmet need(s).

Working with Triggers

We can see triggers as containing two components. The first component is a thought or event. The second component is how we react or respond.

As we have previously discussed, feelings are like messengers, telling us about our needs. In *triggering* situations the messenger is like a rock singer, belting out the message. Also, as we discussed, when we acknowledge the message, the messenger tends to calm down and eventually leaves.

Turning the Light On

When we are triggered, it can be hard to connect to the messenger, because it's hard to connect the message to the current event. For example, I used to get very upset when I got stuck in a long line at a store. I would often tell myself that I *shouldn't* be so upset. I would fight the feeling. That rarely turned out well.

Then, one day as I was standing in line, I asked myself, "What needs of mine are unmet right now?" The answer was effectiveness, choice, and autonomy. When I came up with that answer, suddenly my feelings started to make more sense.

Although being stuck in a line may not be such a horrible thing, my needs for effectiveness, choice, and autonomy are *profound*. People die every day fighting for these needs. They're very important to us humans.

The recognition of these needs helped me gain some perspective. It helped me understand that these needs were very important to me – and since, in my self-empathy, I had identified them, I was able to see that there were other ways that I do meet these needs. In fact, I even began to understand that I was choosing to be *stuck* in lines by choosing to shop in stores that I know get jammed up at times.

When I can "turn the light on" by becoming aware of my needs, it gives me a chance to see that the "monster" is not a monster at all. It's my needs in the dark.

THE CHALLENGE AND OPPORTUNITY

Certainly, working with intense emotions is a challenge. That said, because they are so intense, it becomes pretty easy to know when we are feeling them – and this gives us a cue that we can self-empathize and get a deeper understanding of ourselves. It also gives us a chance to empathize and have a deeper understanding of others who are experiencing intense emotions.

Through this practice we can bring more clarity and compassion into our lives – and that makes life more wonderful.

IN PRACTICE

INVITING A SCARY THING
INTO MY BEDROOM

As a young man and even later in life as an adult, I often experienced a great deal of anxiety when I was alone. I spent many years and dollars trying to figure out a way to stop having this disturbing experience. I believed that this was "an irrational fear" and that I should learn to ignore it.

It wasn't until I had been studying compassionate living that something new happened that changed my life forever. I remember the very moment.

I was lying in bed one night after my girlfriend had left. We had just ended a beautiful and fun weekend together, and she decided that she would prefer to wake up in her own bed – so she left, despite my request that she stay.

I could feel the anxiety coming on. I fought it. In my struggle, I could feel the energy of my fear and anxiety like a storm about to spawn a wicked tornado. I fought some more. My heart began to pound so hard that my chest hurt and my ears were ringing. Then it happened.

In a moment of self-compassion, I became curious about what my feelings were trying to tell me. What was I wanting? What was I feeling? And what important and repeating event did this remind me of?

First, it occurred to me that in this inquiry, I would have to invite this feeling into my body, not fight it. For perhaps the first time in my life, I stopped fighting my fear. I remember thinking, "OK, this won't kill me. Just feel the feeling." I talked to the feeling in my head. "OK, come on over, come in."

In that very moment, I could feel my body start to relax. I was *with* my fear, not fighting it. My heart stopped pounding. I realized that my anxiety was *me*, trying to protect myself from feelings that were profound and frightening to me. I remember becoming grateful for my anxiety and letting it go.

I began to slip into an experience of deep sadness and loneliness. These *new* feelings brought a new awareness. They helped me understand how deeply I was longing for companionship, love, and choice. I realized how I had yearned to have these needs in my life since I was a very young child.

My experience was shifting. Feeling these feelings and connecting to my needs changed everything – right there, instantly and permanently. The world seemed somehow different.

Since that night, I have not once experienced the intense levels of anxiety I used to. On several occasions since then, my anxiety did start to visit. Each time, I invited it in, and in doing so, I could return to a more self-connected state. Being alone is no longer a trigger for me. In fact, I rather like it.

Although I have had success with this particular trigger, I realize that I have plenty more triggers to work through – each one a challenge and an opportunity to make my life more wonderful.

PRACTICES

PRACTICE 1

Finding Your Triggers – Think of a repeating event (or events) in your life where you experience a reaction that seems disproportionate to you, an upset. Then, write down the answers to the following questions:

What is the triggering event? (You can write this as an observation or in the form of a judgment.)

When does it happen?

How does it happen?

Does it happen with a particular person?

What childhood experience(s) does it remind you of?

PRACTICE 2

Working with Your Trigger -— This is a great exercise to do with an empathy buddy. You may want to start with "smaller", less intense triggers if possible and then work your way up to more intense situations.

1) In writing, describe a time when you were upset (triggered).

2) Write down your judgments or the story you are telling yourself about this event.

3) Give yourself empathy or get empathy to identify your feelings and needs in regard to this situation or story.

4) Describe the trigger in pure observation.

5) Give yourself empathy or get empathy again to identify your feelings and needs in this present moment.

6) Connect with the need or needs you have identified by embodying them (see Practice 2, in Chapter 27).

7) Take a few minutes to breathe and think about your experience.

8) See if you have a different perspective about the way these needs show up in your life or if you can think of any requests you might make of yourself or others.

CHAPTER 48

THE CONCEPT

PERVASIVE FEELINGS

As I continue my practice of compassionate living, I am constantly surprised at the limitless depth that is available to me when it comes to connecting with myself, or as we call it, self-empathy.

My self-empathy process almost always begins with an awareness of my feelings. This awareness can be easier when my feelings are obvious, when they are intense or come on quickly. Over time, I have found that it is the subtle and constant feelings that are more difficult to discern.

THE SKILL OF FEELING FEELINGS

As we discussed quite early in the book, *feeling our feelings* is a skill. Many of us have learned to ignore our feelings or push them down below our conscious awareness (see Chapters 3 and 7). In the same way we develop a muscle by repeatedly using it, we can develop our ability to feel feelings by simply turning our attention to them over and over.

Before I started studying compassionate living, I was sure I had two feelings – good and bad. As I began to study and practice, using my Feelings List, I became more *fluent* in my ability to feel and articulate feelings. This, in turn, brought me to a deeper awareness of my needs.

And this allowed me to make requests and make my life more wonderful (see Chapters 13 and 15). Through this skill (or awareness), we can all have an effective perpetual practice of self-compassion and self-compassionate action.

What Are Pervasive Feelings?

It has become clear to me that I am always having some feeling – always. Even in this moment as I type on my keyboard, or as you read this, we are both having some feeling or feelings.

Over the years I've noticed that like fish in water, I can become so accustomed to having certain feelings that I cease to notice them at all. I have learned that these constant *pervasive feelings* are messages, trying to tell me about something, and I am simply not hearing them.

Even a loud message can go unheard if it is constantly there. For example, there was a time when I lived near a train track where trains would constantly pass. I remember when people would come to visit me, we'd be in the yard talking and they would suddenly startle and say, "What was that!?" I would say, "What was what?" "That noise." Then I would realize a train had just passed through and I hadn't even noticed. Feeling our feelings can be just like that.

Listening Inside

There is a depth of *listening* to my feelings that is limitless. This practice of noticing what is happening inside us is a subtle and profound resource we all possess – yet it can escape our awareness. By practicing the simple act of turning our attention inward, we can find wisdom and guidance that has been with us all of our lives. Wisdom that we simply haven't noticed – our feelings – a profound and limitless part of our experience, and a gift that comes with our human lives.

IN PRACTICE

DISCOVERING MY DREAD

Several years ago my Practice Group had been working/playing with our ability to feel our feelings. We were doing some meditations to help us increase our ability to feel our feelings, thereby increasing our awareness of needs (and our choice to make life-serving requests).

One of the practices was to keep a journal of our feelings. One morning, as I was waking up, moving from my sleep state to an awake state, I felt something I had never noticed before. As I reached for my journal, I noticed that a feeling was working its way into my body. In those few seconds between my sleep state and waking state, I caught a glimpse of awareness. It was dread.

In that moment I realized that this feeling of dread had been with me for years. I was shocked and scared, as I saw for the first time, this seemingly massive dark energy alongside me that I had never seen before.

As I lay back down in my bed I slowly shifted from fear to curiosity. What was this dread trying to tell me about? What need was so prevalent and constantly unmet? What need was so profound that it inspired dread? This was a moment of transformation for me. I was entering into an inquiry that would almost assuredly give me a chance to make my life more wonderful.

As the day went on I scanned my consciousness and memory. What was this? By the end of the day I had found it.

I realized that over the past several years my finances had gone from being clear and organized to being ambiguous and disorganized – like a thing in a bad dream that I know is there, yet can't bring myself to look at. By becoming curious, I had found and cracked the code – I discovered a secret that I had been keeping from myself. I was in desperate need for a greater sense of security.

In the coming weeks and months, I paid more attention to creating order and understanding about my finances – and in so doing, addressed my needs for security, order, and peace of mind. Eventually my dread left me. My life became more wonderful.

PRACTICES

PRACTICE 1

Noticing Small Feelings – In a journal, write down how you feel during three uneventful occasions throughout the day. Do this for two or three days. Choose "uneventful" moments. Look for subtle occurrences: someone sneezing, someone saying "I'm next", you saying "thanks", and so on.

This practice helps increase our awareness of feelings by proactively noticing them. Many of us wait until we're "hit over the head" with a feeling before we notice it. By developing the "muscle" of noticing more feelings, we create more opportunities to make our lives more wonderful.

PRACTICE 2

Noticing Pervasive Feelings – In the coming days and weeks keep a small journal by your bedside. As you awaken, check in with yourself. See if you notice any feelings moving into your body and write them down.

Next, if you notice you are experiencing a *pervasive feeling*, see if you can connect it to a *pervasive need*. This step may be more easily accomplished with the support of an empathy buddy.

Finally, if you are able to find the need(s), see if you can think of a request or requests you might make of yourself or others to address them (see Chapters 13 and 15).

CHAPTER 49

THE CONCEPT

CAMPAIGNS

Many of us begin our practice of self-empathy by noticing and identifying a feeling and a need, and then thinking of requests that we hope will contribute to that need being met – and this does work. However, life and self-empathy are not always that simple. Needs can express themselves in *batches* and *layers* (see Chapter 28). As our self-empathy practice deepens and our awareness increases, we have the opportunity to look at a *bigger picture* of our needs and think of more comprehensive ways of addressing them.

THE LAYERING AND BATCHING OF FEELINGS AND NEEDS

As we discussed back in Chapter 28, some needs depend on other needs for their "metness". As you may recall from my story that chapter, my colleague became aware of her need for *order* through an empathy process we did together. After some time and deeper connection, it became clear that she would also love to have more *understanding* and *communication*, as a way to meet her need for order. This deeper awareness brought a sense of hope and creativity that could not come from the awareness of *order* alone.

Our ability to work with multiple feelings and needs can be a game changer, especially when a situation arises that creates *batches* of un-met needs at the same time. For example, if I am having difficulty with my boss at work, my needs for harmony, being seen, and security might all be alive in me.

Understanding and working with the *layering* or *batching* of feelings and needs creates the potential to have more clarity, understanding, and effective compassionate action in our lives.

Understanding my feelings and needs this way allows me to see the bigger, and sometimes confusing, picture of my life, in a new light. It helps me understand my life with more compassion and clarity – and that empowers me to make highly informed requests that make life more wonderful.

CAMPAIGNS

As we discover these *layers* and *batches* of needs, we may find ourselves challenged to make multiple requests. I call this a *campaign*. I use this word because it helps me realize and remember that this is a process – one that could take a while. It may require a sustained focus on my needs, sometimes in a specific sequence.

For example, I might identify a very important and pervasive need – such as *security*. At the same time, I might not know what request(s) to make to address that need directly. With my focus on this need alone, and no requests to make, I could easily give up out of frustration and hopelessness. However, if I can identify my *strategic* (or *prerequisite*) needs for *knowledge* and *understanding* as a way to address my need for *security*, then I can start making requests to address my prerequisite needs (see Chapters 13 and 15). Now I'm on my way to a more wonderful life – moving.

IN PRACTICE

MY JOURNEY TO WATER, ORDER, AND SHELTER

It was fall. The leaves had turned yellow, orange, and burgundy. Winter seemed to be taking its time getting here. It was warm, beautiful, and bright in the Hudson Valley. And yet – I was feeling agitated and uncomfortable, particularly when I was around my home. This was confusing to me because I had just finished an entire round of home improvements – I planted a new garden, planted fruit trees, painted some rooms, and even got some new window treatments. Things were looking good – yet there was something bugging me. I just didn't feel right about my home and I didn't know what to do about it.

At about that same time, my partner asked me if we might do a practice together. She asked if we could review our Needs List together and see how we were doing – kind of an overall inventory. I agreed.

We decided that we would pick the top three needs that we wanted to experience more of. It was an enlightening experience to set aside this time and have this practice of looking at the *big picture* of our lives.

As we went through our list together and thought about each need, one by one, I was quite surprised when we got to *water*, I noticed a bit of unease coming into my body (a messenger). This was confusing at first, because I had a water supply. Then it hit me. I hadn't been drinking water from our tap, because our water supply has a fairly large amount of sulfur in it. And although I had been buying bottled water, I wasn't really enjoying that because it came in plastic bottles and that brought up concern for my health and our environment.

I was surprised, then baffled, because I really didn't have a solution to this problem. I didn't know how to get drinkable water from my tap and I couldn't find a readily available supply in glass containers. I was stumped.

As we continued to go through the list, I was also surprised to discover some unrest when we came across the need for *order*. With some help from my partner, I identified two things. First, I had never unpacked my files when I moved a year and a half earlier, and second, I was still renting a storage space near the place I used to live. I was surprised because both of these things were relatively minor. Yet in the scheme of things, these persisting situations were indeed having an effect on me (see Chapter 48).

I just wasn't feeling great about my home (my need for shelter). I think part of my *unawareness* about this was due to that fact that I do have a tremendous amount of gratitude for my life. That said, order and water are pretty important for me.

That night, my partner made up two little laminated signs for our bathroom mirror, one for each of us. Mine simply said "Order, Water, Shelter".

After that, every morning I would see this little sign with these three words. Thanks to this simple practice, I kept these needs in my awareness.

By the time winter came, I had done some research (needs for knowledge, competence, understanding), designed a relatively inexpensive water filtering system and, with the help of my son, installed it (needs for support and movement). Also, with my son's help, I moved my stuff out of my old storage space and organized it in my basement. After that, I went through my files and got them organized.

To this day, every day, I have cleaner water, more order, and a home that nurtures me.

Although I don't consider this a "dramatic" story, I do consider it an important one. Through empathy and self-empathy, I was able to get clear on some pretty important needs – like water. Instead of giving up because I didn't have an obvious solution, I simply kept my needs in front of me. When I did this, my mind and intuition naturally did the rest. I successfully took care of myself, even though I didn't know how at first.

These subtle yet persistently unmet needs could have easily gone unnoticed. By discovering them and acting on them over time, life got more wonderful.

PRACTICES

PRACTICE 1

Needs Assessment Exercise – Make a copy of the Needs List (see Appendix B).

To the left of each need mark how well that need is currently met in your life from 1 to 10 (1 being not at all, 10 being very satisfied). Next, to the right of each need, mark how important that need is to you (1 being not important and 10 being very important).

Take your time.

> *Note: When you are complete, look for needs with low numbers on the left and high numbers on the right. Most of the time these needs are wonderful candidates for needs campaigns.*

PRACTICE 2

Keep Your Needs in Front of You – Pick the top 3 needs that you would like to experience more "metness" of. Write them on a piece of paper and post it in a place where you will see it every day (bathroom mirror, refrigerator, a door, etc.). If you want to have some fun with this, you can get creative (make collages, laminate it, do some drawing).

Next, identify the need(s) you would have to meet first, in order to meet the original 3 needs you've identified. Give yourself time for this process.

When we give ourselves plenty of space and time for our process, effective strategies become clearer on a physical/feeling level *and* a cognitive level. It is this deeper connection that draws a thread from our feelings, needs, thoughts, and through the world around us. Like turning a large vessel in a new direction, or getting ten people out the door for dinner, this can take time – just keep your list in sight.

Over time, see if you can think of a request or requests you might make of yourself or others (see Chapters 13 and 15). Continue this practice until your life gets more wonderful.

CHAPTER 50

THE CONCEPT

SPEAKING YOUR COMPASSION

Throughout this book we have used specific words as a tool for recognizing the nature of our thoughts, a way to see both the habitual and conscious ways we can think. We have continually used words to bring our awareness to life-energy.

That's why we use the Feelings and Needs List so often in our practice and learning. And although this is a very effective way to develop our consciousness, it can be awkward and even off-putting to others when we speak these words in day-to-day life.

STREET COMPASSION

Many of us try to address this awkwardness by speaking in more traditional or colloquial terms, what we could call *street compassion*.

When we can depart from the specific feeling and need words and express feelings and needs in other, more familiar ways, it can be quite effective in creating more ease and acceptance as we travel our path toward a more compassionate life.

Imagine a friend said to you, "I'm so beat! I don't know what to do next." Then imagine what it would be like if you said, "So I'm guessing you are feeling tired and disheartened because you're needing rest and hope." Hmmmm. Now imagine what it would be like if

288

you said, "Wow. Sounds like you've really got the wind knocked out of your sails."

Someone hearing your first response may be tempted to run away, wondering if you've lost your mind or have been taken over by aliens. Upon hearing the second response, they may sigh and say, "Yeah, it does feel that way." Expressions like the latter come from the awareness of feelings and needs, yet don't necessarily include the specific words — a sweet and natural connection.

THE CHALLENGE

Although speaking in this more "natural" way is something many of us strive for, there are challenges and potential pitfalls to be aware of. As a trainer and teacher I have witnessed over and over again, that when we attempt to speak in this manner early in our learning journey, it often results in a diversion to *habitual thought*. Although we may want this skill right away, it is, in fact, an advanced practice. It calls for preparation and practice if it is to be done in a way that reflects our compassionate consciousness.

As I mentioned earlier, it is the very practice of using specific feeling and need words that helps us create and support the awareness we are seeking. When we use words that we have often used before, they can easily pull our consciousness to old patterns of educating, discounting, analyzing, and a whole host of other less than conscious habitual responses (see Chapter 10). So even though the consciousness we are trying to develop is *ultimately* not about words, it has become clear to me that feeling and need words are *vital* tools that we use to develop and support that consciousness.

So What Can We Do? – Transparency

When I began studying compassionate living and speaking I found myself continually conflicted. I wanted to have the connection that I knew feeling and need words could bring, and at the same time, I knew they were often hard for people to connect to because they were just so different from "normal" speech.

I was worried that if I used this language I would lose friends and alienate family members. This seemed so ironic, because my practice was designed to create *more* connection, and it appeared it could be doing the opposite.

Back then, when I used feelings and need words, I rarely acknowledged that I was being "abnormal". This engendered an experience of *inauthenticity* in the people I was trying to connect with. Eventually it became clear to me that my friends and family were not reacting to the fact that I was doing something very differently, they were reacting to my lack of *transparency* about it. It seemed to them that I was being "fake". Further, since I wasn't checking in with them about it, they were confused as to why I was talking this way. As far as they were concerned, I was analyzing them or "mugging" them with empathy.

This realization allowed me to approach things differently. I learned to become *transparent*. By sharing the fact that I was attempting to interact with them in a new, *abnormal* way, I was able to change our experience.

Today, when I am unable to connect in a colloquial way, I simply say something like, "Can I ask you something that might seem a bit strange?" Much of the time I get a *yes*. Often I get the connection I enjoy so much – and life becomes more wonderful.

IN PRACTICE

YOU WANNA TRY THIS?

After I had been studying compassionate living for a few months I attempted to bring feelings and needs words into my conversations more often. At first, it didn't turn out very well.

I remember one afternoon, I was talking to my son in my office. I was asking him about the cleanliness of his room and when he might be thinking about cleaning it up. At one point he said, "Look, Dad, I'm really busy with other stuff, and it's not a priority for me right now." In hopes of creating more connection, I replied, "So are you feeling overwhelmed and wanting some space?"

Hearing this, he folded his arms in front of him, tipped his head in disgust and said, "You're doing that stuff again, aren't you."

I was. And I realized it wasn't doing anything but creating a deep sense of disconnection. I was stumped, really wondering if this new way of thinking and speaking would ever make a difference in my life. Then it hit me – I just wanted more connection with my son.

"So Collin, look. As you know, I've been studying this stuff for a while and I'm convinced that if we can practice it together, we'll be able to get along better. You wanna try this?"

I was hoping this question would open a dialog. In my mind I was preparing to share the many reasons I had for wanting this practice in our lives. I was preparing to recount the many success stories and concepts I had learned. As I was filling my head in preparation for the ensuing conversation, suddenly, Collin spoke. "OK."

I scrambled to empty my mind of all my preparatory thoughts and come back into the present moment. As I did so, it occurred to me that he had always wanted to get along better, and all he needed was some authenticity. I replied. "Cool."

PRACTICES

PRACTICE 1

Practice Your Street Empathy – This exercise works well with a partner, although you can practice it on your own too.

First, write down something that someone said to you to express some pain or unmet need.

Next, write down the feelings and needs that you imagine they were experiencing.

Then, write down a response that encapsulates or expresses these feelings and needs without actually saying the feeling or need words themselves.

For example: Someone said, "I'm having a crazy week. I can't find time to do anything for myself." Ask yourself, are they frustrated, overwhelmed, stressed out? Do they need balance, space, support? What might you say that would reflect your understanding without using those words?

If you can find a partner to do this with, like an empathy buddy, you can experiment with different phrases and see how they "land".

PRACTICE 2

Practice Your Street Empathy Again – This exercise also works well with a partner, although you can practice on your own too.

First, write down something that someone said to you that expressed some joy or celebration – a met need.

Next, write down the feelings and needs that you imagine they are experiencing.

Then, write down a response that encapsulates or expresses these feelings and needs without actually saying the feeling or need words themselves.

For example: Someone said, "I'm so happy to get some time to myself this weekend." Are they surprised, psyched, jazzed, relieved? Are they getting needs met for balance, space, fun, choice? What might you say that would reflect your understanding without using those words?

As in Practice 1, if you can find a partner to do this with, like an empathy buddy, you can experiment with different phrases and see how they "land".

PRACTICE 3

Getting Transparent – Think of someone in your life with whom you would like to experience more connection and yet feel awkward speaking to in pure feeling and need words.

Get Centered – Give yourself (or get) some empathy about why you would like to speak with them in feeling and need words and also why you are feeling awkward to do so. In other words, get grounded in your needs.

Be Transparent – Explain why you would like to use feeling and need words. Ask what goes on for them hearing your desire. Be prepared to give them empathy and be clear on your willingness to hear *no* to your strategy of using those words (see Chapters 13 and 15).

CHAPTER 51

THE CONCEPT

COMPASSION AS A SPIRITUAL PRACTICE

Note: As I write this, I'm noticing some trepidation in me – some concern about acceptance, and being seen and understood. My intention in writing this is to share my opening and discovery. I don't claim to know "the truth". I am simply sharing some ideas, without expectation or instruction – one account of one human experience, with the hope that it may contribute to you in some way.

It seems that most everyone has a different idea of what the word "spiritual" means. For some, it is the connection to the unknown, a higher power or being, or the divine. For others, it is the connection to one's self. And to yet others, it is the connection to all things.

And so, it seems spirituality is defined universally as a connection to something – the key word being *connection*. For me personally, I have come to define spirituality as the experience of connecting to life, which includes all of the above.

Connection to the Divine

My friend and mentor Marshall Rosenberg used the term "Beloved Divine Energy" to refer to the energy of *life* itself. In his words, "I connect with this energy when I connect to human beings…"

Connection to Self and Others

We could say a spiritual existence is one where we get close to what works for us and stay away from what does not (see Chapter 26). For years, this concept seemed to me to be too simple. As I have practiced compassion, this concept has become more and more meaningful to me.

This simple idea calls on me to self-empathize and consciously connect to my needs. When I nurture myself by nurturing my life-energy (needs), I have found, time after time, that I become curious and inspired to nurture it in others. Alternatively, when I experience disconnection from the life in me, I experience disconnection from the life in others.

The simple practice of seeing my needs gives me a basis to see my actions and the actions of others with compassion. By seeing my own needs and the needs of others, I have a path to compassion even for people (including myself) who have done things that I dislike, or even detest. I have a way to see the disconnection from life-energy as a *tragic event*, not an "evil act" or something that is "wrong".

Through the lens of needs, I always have a way to choose compassion.

Connecting to the Artist through Their Art

The more I practice living in an awareness of the energy of life, the more I feel a connection to that which I cannot see or even conceive of – what I call "The Source". I am certain that I do not understand the nature of the universe. To my mind, there is surely something going on here that is beyond my *comprehension* – yet, it is not necessarily beyond my *experience*.

Through my practice of compassion I increase my experience of the energy of life. Every time I create or facilitate a connection within myself or between human beings, I can feel the partnership with, and an appreciation for, the energy inside every one of us. And in the same way I can experience the beauty of a painting without meeting the artist, I can experience the gift of life, without knowing the source of it.

Although I have never met Picasso or Monet, I am grateful to them for the gift of beauty that I receive when I experience their art. Through my appreciation of the gift of life, I can feel a similar sense of gratitude in every waking moment.

SPIRITUALITY AS ACTION

One of my colleagues recently encouraged me to ask myself what my relationship to life-energy is. Am I its son? Its father? Its friend? Its lover?

I love this question because it helps me think about my role (or roles) in relationship to my life-energy, and to the life-energy around me.

Personally, I have found that I can be a friend to life – all life, in me – in you. As a friend to life, I often ask myself, "What can I do to contribute to you?" or "What can I do to expand and express my appreciation of the things I have been given?" The more I study and practice compassion, the more I can answer these questions.

In my awareness of life (feelings and needs), I can inform my actions (requests) to bring harmony, alignment, and friendship to my life – mutual love and support. My compassion begets the actions of a spiritual existence. Sweet.

IN PRACTICE

THE MISSING PIECE

As a child growing up I was introduced to spirituality through a church. In fact, my grandfather was a minister. Back then, it was explained to me that there was a big gray-haired personage, sitting on a throne, who was in charge of everything. This same person-age created a bunch of rules for me to follow – things that I *should* and *shouldn't* do. And somehow, a certain group of people were in charge of distributing these rules and making sure I followed them. Although I believed this story at first, somehow it never felt right. I spent much of my life confused about this.

I spent many years trying to understand what the meaning of life really was. What was my purpose? Where did I come from? Why am I here? By the time I left college (as a philosophy major) it had become clear to me that I wasn't going to figure these things out with the information that was available to me. I stopped trying.

In 2001, I read the book "Nonviolent Communication: A Language of Life" by Marshall Rosenberg. In this book, I learned that I could choose to see all human actions as an attempt to fulfill our needs. This really resonated with me. I also learned that I could see needs *as* life. Over time, I realized that when I was *in service* to life (needs), I got a deep sense of satisfaction and meaning. I was instinctively drawn to the practice of consciously serving life. I had found a way to be connected to my life in a meaningful, internally sourced way.

Ironically, I found myself interested in doing many of the things I had been told I *should* do earlier in life. Only this time, it was coming from a deep connection to what I *wanted* to do – what fulfilled me.

I can see now, it was the internal connection to my life-energy that was the missing piece all those years before. I was being told to look outside of myself when I was searching for guidance, wisdom, and the source of love. And all the time, it was inside me, just waiting to be found.

PRACTICES

PRACTICE 1

Appreciating Life – This exercise works well if done in solitude, with one or more objects to bring some beauty to the space (a candle, some incense, a picture of someone you love, a flower, or anything else that brings you a sense of beauty).

First, write down 10 things that life is giving you right now. For example, these things might be people, air, a beating heart, comfort, love, food in your stomach, your stomach, your eyes, your sense of smell, your nose, your brain, your mother, your children, your ability to think or read – and so forth.

Then, write down all the different needs that these things meet.

Next, read through your two lists (things and needs).

Finally, close your eyes and scan your body. If you feel some appreciation, simply say or think, "Thank you." Read through your list again and repeat this process for 2 to 3 minutes. Notice what happens inside you.

PRACTICE 2

Contributing to Life – Over the next week, create at least one way, each day, to consciously contribute to life.

This can be donating money to a life-serving organization, watering a plant, opening a door for someone, smiling at a child (or an adult), telling someone to "Keep the change", removing a bug from your home instead of killing it, giving someone flowers or their favorite treat, eating something that is healthy, telling someone what you appreciate about who they are or what they have done (see Chapters 20 and 21 for this last one).

Notice that you are serving life. Notice what happens inside you.

CHAPTER 52

THE CONCEPT

LIVING WITH COMPASSION

"Apathy can be overcome by enthusiasm,
and enthusiasm can only be aroused by two
things: first, an ideal, to take the imagination
by storm, and second, a definite intelligible
plan for carrying that ideal into practice."

— *Arnold J. Toynbee*

As I think back on all the concepts and practices that we have studied together in this book, it becomes clear to me how important it is to have a plan to activate our learning. The following ideas are offered as a way to create a more wonderful life.

HARNESS THE POWER OF YOUR DREAMS

"You are never too old to set another goal or to dream a
new dream."

— *C. S. Lewis*

I have a collection of antique science fiction books. Recently, as I was looking through my collection, I noticed that without exception, everything that was imagined in these books has come to be. From the

"Great Flying Machines" to the "Great War Machines", we humans have created *everything* we have ever imagined. It seems that every human creation starts as an idea, a dream.

As I look at my own life so far, I see how this dynamic applies. Everything I have ever dreamed of has come to be – everything. As I notice this rather astounding phenomenon, I realize how important and powerful my dreams have been – and how important it is to have them.

ANYTHING WORTH DOING IS WORTH DOING POORLY

As we have discussed in previous chapters, we have plenty of practice in *habitual* ways of thinking, speaking, and being (see Chapter 9). If we are to make compassionate thinking and living part of our life, it calls on us to practice and to create new habits – new pathways in our consciousness.

Through practice, we will inevitably see results. The reason I have shared the successes and failures that I have experienced in my pursuit of a compassionate life is to remind you that we will always have failure on our path to success – It's part of the journey. I also wanted to share the sense of beauty and meaning that comes with practice.

GETTING SUPPORT

> *"If you want to travel fast, go alone. If you want to travel far, go together."*
>
> — *African Proverb*

The concepts and practices in this book are not typically supported in our common culture. Many of us are continually supported by our environment to think and behave in ways that do not engender the level of compassion and connection we are capable of experiencing. That's a challenge.

In a way, we can see ourselves as pioneers. Because of this, finding others to share this with becomes vital. In my experience, those of us who find other *like-hearted* folks to practice with have a more fun-filled, effective, and sustainable practice. Finding others to join us on our journey helps us grow and thrive as the interdependent creatures we love to be.

From the first day of my journey, I sought support. To this day, I attend practice groups, workshops, and have weekly calls with my Empathy Buddies. I don't even want to imagine what my life would be like if I did not have this practice in my life. As far as I can tell, we all need support.

Likewise, I have made it a practice to share the concepts and skills of compassion by introducing them to folks who don't know about them yet. Since 2004, I have devoted the first Monday of every month to sharing this work with folks who may not yet know about it or understand it (see Appendix F). This is one of the most rewarding parts of my life. You can share this work as well, by recommending this book or directing people to the resources listed in Appendix F.

IN PRACTICE

FINDING AN ANSWER

When I was twelve years old, I picked up a "Life Magazine" a *coffee table-sized* publication known for its groundbreaking photography. Little did I know that what I was about to see in that magazine would change the course of my life.

As I leafed through the oversized pages, I came across what I can only describe as one of the most horrifying things I have ever seen.

I saw, for the first time in my young life, the reality of war. There was a photo essay on a military action that had taken place in Viet

Nam. Up to that moment, for me, war was a game we played with make-believe guns. No real blood, no real pain, just a game to be won or lost before we headed home for dinner.

As my eyes scanned the pages, my brain was scurrying like a frightened animal. As I took in these images, two things happened. First, I understood that war was a real and horrible reality of my life as a human. And second, I refused to believe it was necessary.

That night, and for several days following, I shared my experience with the "grownups" in my life. They assured me that war was a necessary part of life.

My twelve-year-old mind secretly refused to believe them. And yet, I had no answer to why that was. I looked and I waited for many years.

In 2001, I read the book "Nonviolent Communication: A Language of Life" by Marshall Rosenberg. By the time I had finished reading the first chapter, my wait had ended. In the book, Marshall showed that there are concepts, skills, and practices that we can develop and use to connect with each other. So much so that we can learn to transcend violence.

From then on, I knew exactly what I wanted to do. I began my study of Marshall's work with the most experienced and integrated trainers I could find. It wasn't long before I met Marshall and eventually worked with him as his support person here in New York. During that time I found a new friend and it became clear to me that my future held the potential for a meaningful life, beyond my dreams.

By 2002, I had sold my engineering business, sold my home, and moved to New York City to start The New York Center for Nonviolent Communication.

By 2004, in the process of starting and growing this organization, I had spent every dollar I had. Most everyone was convinced I had lost my mind, with the exception of my parents and my dear friend Nellie (to name the ones I hold the most appreciation for). And maybe I did lose my mind – and found my heart, my dream. I was clear. I was willing to live in a cardboard box if need be, but I could not imagine doing anything besides sharing this work.

I remember one day in particular that year. It was the first Monday of the month and I was especially worried because I was dealing with the reality of my net worth going from six figures to negative six hundred dollars.

That night, I gave my "First Mondays" free introductory workshop, as I had on the first Monday of every month. Afterwards, a woman from a local community service organization asked if she could hire me to teach her and her colleagues. My first paid engagement. I said yes.

The next day (within fourteen hours of the first invitation), I got a call from a member of the Communications Coordination Committee for the United Nations. They, too, wanted to hire me to teach. My dream was becoming a sustainable reality.

Fourteen years later, on a cool sunny Wednesday morning, still in the comfort of my home, I sit down at my computer once again to put the finishing touches on the last chapter of a book I have wanted to write since I was twelve. Thank you for sharing this moment with me.

With tears of gratitude, humility, and awe,

Thom

PRACTICES

PRACTICE 1

Review – You can think of this book as a manual for a life-connected, compassionate existence. Much of the work in this book is what you could call, life work. Even as the author I find it helpful to go back and review these ideas and practices – practices that we will continue to grow in for the rest of our lives.

PRACTICE 2

Connect – As you are reading this, you are in the midst of tens of thousands of folks from around the world who have read this book, who have taken "The Compassion Course Online", or who have participated in my workshops. By connecting to the greater Compassion Course / Book Community you will create a foundation of support that is essential to sustaining a successful practice of compassion in your life.

Use Appendix F in the back of this book to find our online resources, as well as in person trainings, workshops, and events.

I have seen how much individuals and the community at large benefit from this kind of support and mutual companionship.

PRACTICE 3

Dream...

Chapter 52: Living with Compassion

APPENDIX

APPENDIX A – FEELINGS LIST

This list is available in an easily printable version at:
http://compassioncourse.org/feelings.pdf

Feelings Associated with Met Needs

AFFECTIONATE
compassionate
fond
loving
openhearted
tender
warm

ENGAGED
absorbed
curious
engrossed
enchanted
enthralled
entranced

EXHILARATED
enthralled
radiant
electrified
euphoric
overjoyed
thrilled

GRATEFUL
appreciative
moved
thankful
touched
HAPPY
amused

sanguine
up
upbeat

INSPIRED
amazed
eager
enthused
motivated
moved
psyched
stimulated
stirred
wonder

PEACEFUL
calm
comfortable
centered
content
equanimity
fulfilled
mellow
open
quiet
relaxed
relieved
satisfied
serene
tranquil

REFRESHED
recharged
rejuvenated
renewed
rested
restored
revived

blissful
cheerful
delighted
ecstatic

HAPPY
elated
giddy
glad
jolly
joyful
jubilant
merry
overjoyed
pleased
rapturous
tickled

HOPEFUL
confident
expectant
jazzed
lighthearted

fascinated
interested
intrigued
involved
open
spellbound
stimulated

EXCITED
amazed
ardent
aroused
dazzled
energetic
enlivened
enthusiastic
exuberant
invigorated
lively
passionate
surprised
vibrant

Feelings Associated with Unmet Needs

ANGER
aggravated
angry
animosity
annoyed
contempt
disgruntled
enraged
exasperated
furious
hate
hostile
incensed
irate
irritated
irked
livid
miffed
nettled
outraged

mystified
perplexed
puzzled
torn

DISCONNECTION
apathetic
bored
closed
detached
distant
indifferent
listless
numb
withdrawn

DISQUIET
agitated
alarmed
concerned

mortified
self-conscious

FATIGUE
beat
burnt out
depleted
exhausted
listless
pooped
sleepy
tired
weary
wiped out
worn out

FEAR
afraid
anxious
apprehensive

dread
fearful
foreboding
frightened
guarded
insecure
leery
mistrustful
panicked
petrified
scared
shaky
terrified
trepidation
wary
worried

PAIN
aching
agony

peeved
resentful

AVERSION

abhorrence
appalled
bothered
displeased
disgust
dislike
enmity
horrified
loathing
repulsion
revulsion

CONFUSION

ambivalent
baffled
bewildered
conflicted
dazed
discombobulated
disoriented
mixed

distraught
disconcerted
dismayed
disturbed
frustrated
perturbed
rattled
restless
shocked
startled
surprised
troubled
turbulent
turmoil
uncomfortable
uneasy
unnerved
unsettled
upset

EMBARRASSMENT

ashamed
chagrined
discomfited
flustered

anguished
devastated
grief
heartbroken
hungry
hurting
lonely
miserable
regretful
remorseful

SADNESS

depressed
dejected
despairing
despondent
disappointed
discouraged
disheartened
forlorn
gloomy
heavy hearted
hopeless
melancholy
miserable

unhappy
wistful

TENSION

anxious
closed
distressed
edgy
fidgety
frazzled
frustrated
jittery
nervous
overwhelmed
restless
stressed out

YEARNING

longing
nostalgic
pining

Appendix B – Needs and Values: Things We All Want in Our Lives

This list is available in an easily printable version at:

http://compassioncourse.org/needs.pdf

AUTONOMY
choice
dignity
freedom
independence
self-expression
space
spontaneity

CONNECTION
acceptance
affection
appreciation
authenticity
belonging

self-connection
self-expression
shared
reality stability
support
to know and be known
to see and be seen
trust
understanding
warmth

MEANING
awareness
celebration
challenge

PEACE
acceptance
balance
beauty
communion
ease
equanimity
faith
harmony
hope
order
peace-of-mind
space

care
closeness
communication
communion
community
companionship
compassion
consideration
empathy
friendship
inclusion
inspiration
integrity
intimacy
love
mutuality
nurturing
partnership
presence
respect/self-respect
security
self-acceptance
self-care

clarity
competence
consciousness
contribution
creativity
discovery
efficiency
effectiveness
growth
integration
integrity
learning
mourning
movement
participation
perspective
presence
progress
purpose
self-expression
stimulation
understanding

PHYSICAL WELL-BEING

air
care
comfort
comfort
food/nutrition
movement/exercise
rest/sleep
safety (physical)
self-care
sexual expression
shelte
touch
water

PLAY

adventure
excitement
fun
humor
joy
relaxation
stimulation

Appendix C - Shifting Toward Compassion Exercise

Note: this exercise is available online at http://theexercise.org. It includes, hyperlinks, and lists so that you can do the exercise anytime, anywhere.

I created this exercise so people can have what I call a "shift". In other words, a shift in what you are thinking about and how you feel. To understand "shift," I have found it helpful to imagine a line like the one below labeled "Connection Continuum". On one end is rage, disconnection, and violence… on the other is compassion, connection, and peace. In any given moment we are all somewhere on this line (many or most of us in the middle somewhere).

The Connection Continuum

<<< You and me (always moving back and forth) >>>

_____

rage, disconnection, violence << >> connection, compassion, peace

The Key

When we interact with other people, we are constantly moving back and forth on this line, often from moment to moment, at times even second to second. This exercise is a tool to move yourself toward a more compassionate state, even in difficult moments.

The Exercise

You can increase your benefit by taking your time, reading it completely, and following the hints. You can do "The Exercise" as many times as you like and keep using it with different situations.

Before You Begin

1) You will need a pen or pencil and a piece of paper with a blank side.

2) We will be using the Feelings and Needs Lists in this book (see appendices A and B).

3) Leave yourself an uninterrupted twenty to thirty minutes. This exercise can require a fair amount of concentration.

Step 1

Take a blank side of paper and at the top, write down something somebody said to you that you *didn't* like hearing.

Hints:

1) People who choose a less than traumatic, yet "stimulating", situation seem to have greater success early on.

2) Think of the exact quote. No story line or background is needed for this exercise, just the quote.

STEP 2

Now draw a "T" shape on the top half of the paper, large enough to write two columns of words. Put an "F" above the left column and an "N" above the right column.

STEP 3

On the left side, under the "F" column, write down how you're feeling when you think about that quote. Use the Feelings List from Appendix A.

STEP 4

On the right side, under the "N" column, write down what you are (or were) needing and not getting, the moment you heard the words. Use the Needs List from Appendix B.

STEP 5

Take a minute [...] close your eyes, and relax. After some time, look at the list again. If you feel certain this list represents what you were experiencing then go to Step 6. If you feel like something's missing, go back to the Feelings and Needs Lists and look again until you have a sense of completion.

STEP 6

Draw a second "T" shape on the bottom half of the paper, with an "F" on the left side and an "N" on the right, just like before.

STEP 7

On the left side, under the "F" column, write down what you *imagine* the other person was feeling when you heard what they said. If you really can't think of what they were feeling, you can try going back to Step 5 and double-checking your own list. Most people have difficulty completing Step 7 until their *own* list is really complete.

STEP 8

On the right side, under the "N" column, write down what you *imagine* the other person was needing and not getting in the moment you heard their words. Just like Step 7, if you really can't think of what they were needing, you can try going back to Step 5 and double checking your own list. Most people have difficulty doing Step 8 until their own list is really complete.

STEP 9

Take a minute [...] close your eyes, and relax. After some time, look at all the lists (your feelings and needs, their feelings and needs). If you feel comfortable these lists represent what both of you were experiencing, then go to Step 10. If you feel like something's missing, go back and look at all the lists again, until you are sure they are as complete as you can get them.

STEP 10

Again, take a minute [...] Check in with yourself and see if you notice a shift in how you feel about what was said to you, or how you feel toward the person that said it. Do you have a way of thinking about this that wasn't there before? Do you feel more connected than when you started? If you do, then you've had a shift. You've consciously moved yourself toward compassion. It is this very aspect – that a shift can occur based on how you think versus what happened – that makes this work so powerful. It means that, in its most developed state, we can proactively pursue a connection – even with people who have done things that we find abhorrent.

If you feel the same or worse you may want to try again with the same quote or one on a subject that's not as "hot" for you. Please note: About twenty percent of people that do the exercise *do not* shift on the first time through. One hundred percent of people, who keep trying, eventually do.

Last Hint: *People who practice this over and over report more success in "shifting". It's like developing a muscle.*

Appendix D – Non-Feeling Word Game

Use each of these "non-feeling words" in a sentence. Then, check your Feelings and Needs Lists and see if you can figure out which feelings and needs are associated with each "non-feeling word".

abandoned
abused
attacked
belittled
betrayed
blamed
bullied
caged/
boxed in

cheated
coerced
cornered
criticized
discounted
diminished
disliked
distrusted
dumped on

harassed
hassled
ignored
insulted
interrupted
intimidated
unaccepted

Appendix E – Translating Judgments Into Observations Exercise

Keys

Anger, judgment, demand and other forms of right/wrong thinking are all an expression of feelings and needs.

When we are starting to feel a sense of disconnection, we can connect with our feelings and needs, noticing what we are wanting, wanting more of what we value, as opposed to focusing on blame or judgment.

By making judgment free observations associated with clearly identified needs, we are more likely to re-establish a level of connection that will lead to everybody's needs being considered.

Begin with any of the statements that you relate to most from the statements below or write your own if you'd rather. Imagine each statement is something that you might want to say to another person. In this exercise you will first, identify your judgment thought, then translate the statements into feelings, needs, and observations. Use the Feelings and Needs Lists.

Don't ever lie to me about where you went.

What is my right/wrong or should/shouldn't thought?

I feel:

Because I need:

I see/hear:

YOU'RE JUST NOT PUTTING IN YOUR SHARE OF THE WORK.

What is my right/wrong or should/shouldn't thought?

I feel:

Because I need:

I see/hear:

THIS PLACE IS A MESS!

What is my right/wrong or should/shouldn't thought?

I feel:

Because I need:

I see/hear:

YOUR OWN

What is my right/wrong or should/shouldn't thought?

I feel:

Because I need:

I see/hear:

Appendix F – Ways to Connect

About the Book and the Course

http://compassionbook.org

http://compassioncourse.org

Finding an Empathy Buddy

http://nycnvc.org

International Educational Network

http://nycnvc.org

http://practicegroups.org

Made in the USA
Las Vegas, NV
08 June 2023

73135939R00196